Key Documents to Understanding the Great Apostasy

Compiled by

Brother Hermengild T.O.S.F.

Table of Contents

Introduction..5

Sermon of Saint Jerome..6

They Have Taken Away My Lord...7

Permanent Instruction Of The Alta Vendita............................27

A Catholic Utopia...33

Lecture on the Great Apostasy given by Henry Edward Cardinal
Manning...39

The Jewish Peril and the Catholic Church...............................59

Vision of Pope Leo XIII...64

Truth About The Devil...67

The Real Story Of AA - 1025...87

Concluding Thoughts..102

Recommended Books For Further Study................................104

Introduction

We have included here in the order of their publication documents that are key to understanding the Great Apostasy. These are lesser known, but very important documents on this subject. There are also books that will help in further in depth study of this question. These documents have circulated publicly and privately over the last half a century and more and are deemed important to this understanding.

Pope Saint Pius X in <u>Pascendi</u> warned: "That We should act without delay in this matter is made imperative especially by the fact that the partisans of error are to be sought not only among the Church's open enemies; but, what is to be most dreaded and deplored, in her very bosom, and are the more mischievous the less they keep in the open. We allude, Venerable Brethren, to many who belong to the Catholic laity, and, what is much more sad, to the ranks of the priesthood itself, who, animated by a false zeal for the Church, lacking the solid safeguards of philosophy and theology, nay more, thoroughly imbued with the poisonous doctrines taught by the enemies of the Church, and lost to all sense of modesty, put themselves forward as reformers of the Church; and, forming more boldly into line of attack, assail all that is most sacred in the work of Christ, not sparing even the Person of the Divine Redeemer, whom, with sacrilegious audacity, they degrade to the condition of a simple and ordinary man." (It is recommended to undertake a study of this important document.)

Let us remember as Saint Paul said in Second Thessalonians, "the mystery of iniquity worketh already". Indeed in studying these documents the plans of the conspiracy to attempt to destroy the Catholic Church will become quite clear. These documents are presented without further comment, so that you can draw your own conclusions.

We recommend taking notes as you read.

Brother Hermenegild.

Sermon of Saint Jerome

This injunction to whoso readeth, to understand, sheweth that there is here something mysterious. In Daniel we read as followeth : And in the midst of the week the sacrifice and the oblations shall be taken away ; and in the temple there shall be the abomination of desolation, even until the consummation of the time ; and a consummation shall be given to the desolation. It is of this same thing that the Apostle speaketh, when he saith that a man of iniquity, even an adversary, shall be exalted against whatsoever is called God, or is worshipped : so that he shall even dare to stand in the temple of God, and to shew himself as God ; whose coming shall, according to the working of Satan, destroy and banish from God all who shall receive him.

This prophecy may be understood either (first) simply of Antichrist, (secondly) of the statue of Caesar, which Pilate set up in the Temple, or (thirdly) of the statue of Hadrian on horse-back, which hath stood, even until our own day, upon the site of the Holy of Holies. In the Scriptures of the Old Testament Abomination is a word very often used for an idol, and the farther title Of Desolation is added to identify an idol erected upon the site of the desolate and ruined temple.

The abomination of desolation can be taken to mean as well every perverted doctrine. When we see such a thing stand in the holy place, that is in the Church, and pretend that it is God, we must flee from Judea to the mountains, that is, departing from the letter of the law which kills, and from Jewish distortions of the law, we must draw near to the eternal mountains where God shines wondrously. We must be on a housetop and in a house where the fiery darts of the devil cannot reach us. We must not come down and carry with us anything from the house of our old manner of life, nor seek the things we left behind. Rather we are to sow in the field of the spiritual scriptures to read a harvest from them. Neither shall we take another cloak. Such things are forbidden Apostles.

They Have Taken Away My Lord

"...they have taken away my Lord."
(John 20:13)

by Fr. Demaris

-Translated from French by A. Drover

The time is coming when Catholics may not have good true priests to say the Mass and to administer the Sacraments. This has happened before and the following is a letter to the faithful explaining their plight and how to overcome it. It is written by Father Demaris, Professor of Theology, Missionary of St. Joseph at Lyon in 1801 under these identical circumstances.

Dear Children,

In the midst of human vicissitudes and the havoc of shock to the feelings, you voice your fears to your father and ask for a Rule of conduct. I'm going to show you and try to instill into your souls the consolation you need.

Jesus Christ, the model for Christians, teaches us by His conduct, what we must do in the painful situation in which we find ourselves, and St. Luke tells us (Ch. 13) that some Pharisees, coming to Our Lord, said "Go away from here, Herod wants to have you put to death". He answered, "Go tell that fox that I have yet to chase out demons and give health to the sick, today and tomorrow and the third day my life shall be finished. Anyway, I must carry on today and tomorrow and the next day and a prophet must die only at Jerusalem."

You are frightened, my children, at what you see: all that you hear is frightening: but be consoled that it is the will of God being accomplished: your days are numbered, His Providence watches over us.

Cherish those men who appear to you as savages, they are the means which Heaven uses in its plans, and like a tempestuous sea, they will not pass the prescribed line against the countering and menacing waves.

The stormy turbulence of revolution which strikes right and left, and the sounds which alarm you are the threats of Herod! Let it not deter you from good works, nor change your trust, nor wither the shower of virtues which tie you to Jesus Christ. He is your Model, and the threats of Herod do not change the course of His Destiny.

I know you can be deprived of your freedom, that one can even seek to kill you. I would say then what St. Peter said to the first faithful, "What pleases God is, that with a view to pleasing Him we should endure all the pain and suffering given to us unjustly."

What glory would you have if it were for your sins you endured maltreatment? But if in doing good you suffer with patience, that is pleasing to God. For this is why you have been called, since Jesus Christ has suffered for us, leaving you an example to follow. He, Who had committed no sin, Whose Mouth no wrong had spoken, when heaped with curses gave none in return, when ill-treated made no threats, but gave Himself into the hands of one who judged Him unjustly." (Peter, Ch. 2 v. 19/23.)

The disciples of Jesus Christ in their fidelity to God are faithful to their country and full of submission and respect for all authority, firm in their principles with a conscience without reproach, adoring the Will of God, they mustn't cowardlike flee persecution; when one loves the Cross, one is fearless to kiss It and even enjoy death. It is necessary for our intimate union with Jesus Christ. It could happen any instant but it is not always so meritorious or glorious. If God does not call you to it, you shall be like those illustrious confessors of whom St. Cyprian said, "that without dying by the executioner they have gained the merits of martyrdom, because they were prepared for it."

The conduct of St. Paul mentioned in Acts of the Apostles, Ch. 20-21, tells us how one must model oneself on Jesus Christ. "Going to Jerusalem, he learnt at Caesarea that he would be persecuted there. The faithful besought him to avoid going, but he believed himself called to be crucified with Jesus Christ if such was His wish, and his only reply to them was, "Stop softening my heart with your tears. I tell you I am prepared to suffer at Jerusalem, not only prison, but even death for Jesus Christ."

There, my children, such must be your dispositions: the shield of faith must arm you, hope must sustain you and charity guide you in everything. If, in all and always we must be simple as the doves and prudent as the serpents, it must be above all that we are afflicted for Jesus Christ. I will recall for you here a maxim of St. Cyprian which in these times must be the rule of your faith and piety: "Don't seek too much," said this illustrious martyr, "the chance of a fight: and don't dodge it too much. Let us await God's command and let us hope for His Mercy alone. If God asks of us a humble confession rather than a fierce protestation, then humility is our greatest strength."

This saying invites us to mediate on the strength, the patience and the joy with which the Saints suffered. Look at what St. Paul said and you'll be convinced that when one is animated by faith, troubles only afflict us outside and are but an instrument of battle which victory crowns. This consoling truth can only be appreciated by the righteous, and don't be surprised if in our own time, we see what St. Cyprian saw in his (during the first persecution) that most of the faithful succumbed.

To love God and fear Him alone, such is the apanage of a small number of the elect. It is this love and this fear which makes martyrs by detaching the faithful from the world and attaching them to God and His Holy Law.

To support this love and this fear, in your hearts, watch and pray. Increase your good works and join to that the edifying acts of which the first faithful have given us example. Mix with followers of the Faith and then glorify the Lord as did the first Christians whom we retrace in the fourth chapter of the Acts of the Apostles.

This practice will be much more salutary seeing that you are deprived of ministers of the Lord who nourished your souls with Bread of the Word. You weep for these men precious to your piety. I appreciate all your loss. You feel lonely by yourselves, but couldn't this loneliness be salutary to you in the eyes of faith? It is by faith that the faithful are united. In probing this truth, we find that the absence of the body doesn't break this unity, since it doesn't break the ties of faith, but rather augments it by depriving it of all feeling.

Christians who live only by faith, are united by faith alone. If you were united by those ties to the ministers of the Lord whom you regret, console yourselves: their absence purifies and enlivens the love which unites us. Faith renders present for us, those whom we love in relation to our salvation, whatever the distance and chains which separate us. Faith gives us eyes so piercing that we can see them wherever they are, when they are at the ends of the earth, and when death has separated them from the world. Nothing is far away in Faith. It plumbs the depths of the earth as the heights of the heavens. Faith is beyond the senses and its empire beyond the power of men.

Who can prevent us loving whom we wish?

Who can steal from us, memory?

Who can prevent us from presenting to God with those we love, and asking Him for our daily bread, by prayers in union with those whom we love?

It is not enough, my children, to console you on the absence of the Lord's ministers and to dry the tears you shed on their chains. This loss deprives you of Sacraments and spirirual consolation.

Your piety takes fright, it sees itself alone. However just your desolation, never forget that God is your Father, and if He permits your deprivation of the dispensation of the mysteries, that doesn't mean that He shuts off the means of His Graces and Mercies. I'm going to offer them to you as the only sources to which you can possibly go for purification.

Read what I write with the same intention as I have in writing. Seek nothing but the Truth and our salvation in self-denial, in our love for God and a perfect submission to His Holy Will.

Sacraments

You know of the efficacy of the Sacraments, you know of the obligation imposed on you to have recourse to the Sacrament of Penance to cleanse us of our sins. But to profit from these channels of mercy, it requires ministers of the Lord.

In our position, without worship, without Altar, without Sacrifice, without priests, we only see Heaven and no longer have mediators among men.

Let this abandonment not deject us!

We offer Faith to Jesus Christ our Immortal Mediator.

He reads our hearts, He understands our desires, He will crown our faithfulness.

We are, in the eyes of His All-powerful Mercy, this sick one of thirty-eight years old, to whom He said to cure, not to get someone to put him in the bath, but to take up his bed and walk.

If life's events change the position of the faithful, the events change our obligations. Once upon a time we were servants who received five talents, we had the peaceful exercise of our religion.

Today we have but one talent, our heart.

Let us make it fruitful and our recompense will be equal to that of five.

God is just. He doesn't ask of us the impossible.

But because He is just, He asks of us fidelity in all that is possible.

Respectful to the divine and ecclesiastical laws which recall us to the Sacrament of Penance, I must tell you, that in these circumstances, these laws DO NOT OBLIGE.

Listen to what I tell you.

It is essential for your learning and consolation that you should know these circumstances, in order to NOT ACCEPT YOUR OWN MIND FOR THAT OF GOD.

The circumstances where these laws do not oblige, are those where God's Will manifests itself to obtain our salvation without the intermediary of man.

God needs nobody but Himself to save us when He so desires.

He is the Source of life and He gives to everyone the ordinary means that He has provided to effect our salvation: by extraordinary means that His Mercy dispenses us according to our needs.

He is a loving father who by ineffable means helps His children, when believing themselves abandoned, they seek Him and yearn for Him.

If in the course of our lives we had in the least neglected the means which God and His church had provided for our sanctification, we would have been ungrateful children, but if we were to believe that in the extraordinary circumstances we couldn't do without even greater means, we would be forgetting and insulting the Divine Wisdom Who puts us to the test, and Who, in wishing us to be deprived of it, makes it up to us with His Spirit.

Rule of Conduct

To show you, my children, your exact rule of conduct, I am going to apply to your situation, the principles of Faith, and some examples of the history of religion which should develop all the senses and console you in the use you are able to make of them.

It is of Faith, the first and most necessary of all Sacraments, BAPTISM! It is the doorway of salvation and eternal life. However, the desire, the wish for Baptism suffices in certain cases. Catechumens who were surprised by persecution, only received it in blood which they spilt for religion. They found the grace of all the Sacraments in the free confession of their faith, and they were received into the Church by the Holy Ghost, Who is the tie which unites all the members to the Head.

It was thus the martyrs saved themselves, their blood serving as Baptism: it will be thus that will be saved all those who, instucted in our mysteries, shall desire, according to their faith, to receive them.

Such is the law of the church, founded on what St. Peter said that one cannot refuse the water of Baptism to those who have received the Holy Ghost.

When one has the Spirit of Jesus Christ, one cannot be separated from Jesus Christ. When we are persecuted for love of Him, deprived of all help, heaped with captive's chains, when we are led to the scaffold, we then have all the Sacraments in the Cross. This Instrument of our redemption embraces all that is necessary for our salvation.

The tradition and history of the better days of the Church, confirm this dogmatic truth. The faithful who desired the Sacraments, the confessors and martyrs were saved without Baptism and without any Sacrament, since they couldn't received them. From that it is simple for us to conclude that no Sacrament is necessary when it is impossible to receive it, and this conclusion is the belief of the Church.

St. Ambrose regarded the pious Emperor Valentinian as a Saint, although he died without the baptism he desired, but which he hadn't been able to receive. "It is the DESIRE and the WILL which saves us in this case," said the Doctor of the Church, "he who doesn't receive the Sacraments from the hand of men, receives them from God: who is not baptised by men, is baptised by his piety, is baptised by Jesus Christ."

What this great man said of Baptism, let us say of all the Sacraments, of all the ceremonies, and all the prayers that we can be deprived of at the present time.

He who is unable to go to confession to a priest, but who, having all the necessary dispositions for the Sacrament, the desire, and in form the most firm and constant wish, hears Jesus Christ who, touched and witness to his faith, says to him or her what He once said to the sinning woman, "Go, it is forgiven you because you have loved much."

St. Leo said that love of justice contains in itself all apostolic authority, and in that he has expressed the belief of the Church.

Confession

The application of this maxim has place for all like ourselves, who are deprived of apostolic ministry by persecution which removes or incarcerates all true ministers of Jesus Christ worthy of the faith and piety of the faithful.

It has place above all if we are stricken with persecution, we suffer then for justice.

The Cross of Christ leaves no blemish when embraced and carried as It should be. Here, instead of reasoning, let us listen to the language of Saints.

The confessors and martyrs of Africa, writing to St. Cyprian, said boldly that one renewed one's conscience pure and spotless in the Courts when one had confessed the Name of Jesus Christ.

They didn't say that one went there with a pure conscience.

Nothing silences measures which are the tests of Saints, if we cannot confess our sins to priests, confess them to God.

I feel, my children that your worry and scruples are vanishing and that your faith and love of the Cross is increasing.

Say to yourselves, and by your conduct say to all who see you, what St. Paul said: "Who can separate me from the love of Jesus Christ? Shall it be tribulation, hunger, nudity, etc." (Romans 8)

St. Paul then, was in position and he didn't say that any minister of the Lord, where he was able to find one, would be able to separate him from Jesus Christ and change his love for Him. He knew that, robbed of all human help and deprived of an intermediary between himself and Heaven, he found in his love, his zeal for the Gospel and in the Cross, all the Sacraments and means of salvation necessary.

From what I have just said, it is easy for you to see a great truth, proper to your consolation and to give you courage: it is that your conduct is a true confession before God and before men.

If Confession must precede Absolution, your conduct here, precedes the graces of holiness and justice which God gives you, and is a Confession public and continuous.

"Confession is necessary," said St. Augustine, "because it embraces the condemnation of sin."

Here, we condemn it in a manner so public and so solemnly, that it is known by all, and this condemnation which is why we cannot go to a priest, isn't it more meritorious than an accusation of private sin made in secret? Isn't it more satisfactory and edifying? The secret condemnation of our sins to a priest costs us little, while this which we make today is supported by the general sacrifice of our possessions, of our liberty, of our rest, of our reputation and perhaps even of our life.

The confession we'd be making to the priest would only benefit ourselves, while that which we presently make is useful to our brothers and can serve all the Church. God confers on us, unworthy as we are, the grace of wanting to use us to show that it is an enormous crime to offend against truth and justice, and our voice shall be much more intelligible when we suffer greater evils with more patience.

Our example tells the faithful that there is more evil than one thinks in doing what is done to us. We do not confess to a priest, but we confess to the truth, which is the most noble confession, and the most necessary in these circumstances.

We don't confess our sins in secret, we confess the truth in public.

We are persecuted, the truth is not captive and we have this consolation in the hope that we suffer, that we don't hold back God's truth in injustice, as the Apostle of the nations says, and that we teach our brothers not to hold it back.

Finally, if we don't confess our sins, the Church confessed them for us.

Such are the admirable rules of Providence, which allows these trials to make us obtain merit and make us reflect seriously on the use we have made of the Sacraments

The habit and ease that we had for confession often made us lukewarm: instead of as at present, deprived of confessor, one turns in on oneself, and the fervour increases. Let us look at this privation as a fast for our souls and a preparation to receive the bread of penance which, greatly desired, will become a more salutary nourishment.

Strive to banish from our conduct, which is our confession before men and our accusation before God, all the faults which might have crept into our ordinary confessions, above all, the paucity of interior humility.

What I have said is more than sufficient.

However, I am not sure that I have been able to transquilise you on the anxieties and scruples which are conjured up in a soul which has to judge itself, and to follow its own directions. I sense, my children all the importance of your solicitude, but when one trusts in God, one mustn't do it by halves as this would show lack of confidence, as looking at the extraordinary means by which God calls and keeps His elected in justice, as incomplete and leaving something to desire in the order of grace.

You found in the wisdom, maturity and experience of ministers of the Lord, advice and wise practices for avoiding sin, to do good and gain in virtue. All that was not of a sacramental character, but of private enlightenment. A virtuous, zealous, enlightened, charitable friend, cold on this point be your judge and guide. Pious persons did not go to the tribunal of penance only for instruction and enlightenment. They opened their hearts to illustrious people by their holiness in their intimate discussions.

Do the same, but let the most discreet charity reign in these mutual interchanges of your souls, of your wills and desires. God will bless them and you will find there the guidance you need. If this means is not open to you , rely on the mercy of God. He will not abandon you. His Spirit Itself will inflame and direct them towards the high objectives of your destiny.

You are finding me concise on this subject, your desires go well beyond, but have patience and the rest will thoroughly answer your expectations. One can't say everything at once, especially on such a delicate matter which demands the greatest exactitude. I'm going to continue talking to you as I talk to myself.

Removed from the resources of the Sanctuary, and deprived of all exercise of the priesthood, there remains no mediator for us, save Jesus Christ. It is to Him we must go for our needs. Before His Supreme Majesty we must bluntly tear the veil off our consciences, and in the search of good and bad that we shall have done, thank Him for His Graces, confess our sins and ask His pardon and to show us the direction of His Holy Will, having in our hearts the sincere desire to do it to His minister, whenever we are able to do so.

There, my children, is what I call confessing to God!

In such a confession well made, God Himself will absolve us.

It is the Gospel which teaches this to us, in giving us the example of the Publican, who, humiliating himself before God, went away justified, since the best sign of absolution is justice, which cannot be tied, because it unties (looses).

So in the total isolation in which we find ourselves, that is what we must do.

Holy Scripture here outlines our duties.

All which attaches to God is holy.

When we suffer for the truth, our sufferings are those of Jesus Christ, who honours us then with a special character of resemblance to Him with His Cross. This grace is the greatest happiness which could possibly happen to a mortal in this life. It is thus in all painful situations which deprive us of the Sacraments, the carrying of the Cross like a Christian is the source of the remission of our sins, such as once carried by Jesus Christ, it was for the sins of the whole human race. To doubt this truth is to wound the crucified Savior. It is to confess that one does not realise deeply enough the virtue and merits of the Cross.

Tell me, would it be possible that the Good Thief received on it the forgiveness of all his sins, and the faithful one who gives up everything for God, should not by it be forgiven his?

The holy fathers observe that the Thief was a thief right to the Cross to show the faithful what they must hope for from this Cross when they embrace it, and remain attached to it for justice and truth.

Jesus ending His Sufferings entered Heaven by the Cross.

To be sanctified by the Cross our actions must reflect the virtue of Jesus. It is not sufficient in these times, that animated with His love, like St. John you rest your head on His breast. You must serve Him with firmness and constancy, on Calvary and on the Cross. There, in confessing to God, if your confession is not crowned by the imposition of the hands of the priest, it will be by the imposition of the hands of Jesus Christ. See those adorable hands which appeared so heavy by nature, and which are so light to those who love Him. They are spread over you from morning till night, to heap you with all sorts of blessing like that of Christ crucified, when He blesses His children from the Cross.

The Sacrament of Penance is for us at this moment like the Well of Jacob, whose water is pure and salutary, but the well is deep. Without anything we are unable to draw from it and slake our thirst: there are even guards to prevent entry: that is the picture of our position. Look at the action of our persecutors as a punishment for our sins. It is certain that if we could approach the well with faith, we would find Jesus there talking to the Samaritan woman. But don't be discouraged, let us go down in the valley of Bethulie where we'll find several springs which are not guarded, where we can leisurely quench our thirst. Let Jesus Christ live in our heart and His Holy Ghost inflame it, and we'll find in ourselves that spring of living water which gives life and makes up for Jacob's Well. As Sovereign Pontiff, Jesus Christ Himself, does in an ineffable manner in the confession which we make to God, that which in other times He would have done by the advantage which men can not take away. So carrying Jesus in us, Who looks after us continually, we can do it any time, any place and in any disposition. It is something worthy of admiration and recognition to see that what the world does to us to drive us away from God and His Christ, only brings us closer.

Confession mustn't be only a remedy for past sins, but must be a preservative for sins to come. If we seriously reflect on this double efficacy of the Sacrament of Penance, we are able to have much to humiliate us and to bewail, and we shall be so much better founded in it, that our advancement for virtue shall have been slower, and that we shall be found the same still before and after confession, we are able now to repair these faults, which came from too great a trust in Absolution and that one didn't examine thoroughly enough one's weaknesses. Obliged to bewail now before God, the faithful soul considers all its deformities, and there at the feet of our Savior, stricken with the grief of repentance, it remains there silent, only speaking with tears as did the sinning woman of the Gospel. Seeing on the one hand all her wretchedness and on the other the goodness of God, she prostrated herself before His Majesty until her sins were cleansed by one of His looks. That is how the Divine Light enlightens a contrite and humble heart right to the particles which can darken it.

Let this confession to God be for you a short daily practice, but fervent, and that from time to time you do it from one epoch to another as you have been doing it daily. The first fruit you will draw from it, apart from the remission of your sins, will be to learn to know yourself and to know God, the second will be, to be ever ready to present yourself to a priest, if you are able, enriched in character by the mercy of the Lord.

I think I have said all that I should have, my children, on your actions during privation of the Sacrament of Penance.

I'm going to discuss now the privation of that of the Eucharist and after that all those things you mentioned in your letter.

The Eucharist

The Eucharist had for you many joys and advantages when you were able to participate in this Sacrament of love, but now that you are deprived of it for being defenders of truth and justice, your advantages are the same, for who would have dared approach this fearsome table if Jesus Christ had not given us a precept and if the Church, which desires that we fortify ourselves with this bread of life, had not invited us to eat it by the voice of its ministers, who re-clothed us with a nuptial dress.

All was obedience, but if we compare obedience by which we are deprived of with that which led us there, it will be easy to judge the merit.

Abraham OBEYED in immolating his son, and in NOT immolating him, but his OBEDIENCE was greater when he took the sword in his hand than when he returned it to its scabbard. We are OBEDIENT in going to Communion, but in holding ourselves from the Sacrifice we are immolating ourselves.

Quenched of the thirst of justice and depriving ourselves of the Blood of the Lamb which alone can slake it, we sacrifice our own life as much as it is in us to do.

The sacrifice of Abraham was for an instant, an angel stopped the knife, ours is daily, renewing itself every day, every time that we adore with submission the Hand of God which drives us away from His Altars, and this sacrifice is voluntary.

It is to be advantageously deprived of the Eucharist, to raise the standard of the Cross for the cause of Christ and the glory of His Church. Observe, my children, that Jesus, after having given His Body, found no difficulty in dying for us.

There is the action of a Christian in the persecutions, the Cross follows on from the Eucharist. Let not the love of the Eucharist drive us away from the Cross.

It is to arise and make glorious advance in the grace of the Gospel, to go out from the Cenacle, to go to Calvary. Yes, I have no fear in saying it.

When the storm of the malice of men roars against truth and justice, it is more advantageous to the faithful to suffer for Christ than to participate in His Body by Communion.

I seem to hear the Saviour saying to us, "Don't be afraid to be separated from My table for the confession of My Name: it is a grace I give you, which very rare. Repair by this humiliating deprivation which glorifies Me, all the Communions which dishonour me. Feel this Grace. You can do nothing for me and I put into your hands a means of doing what I have done for you, and to return to me with magnificence, that which I have given you greatest.

"I have given you my Body, and you give It back to Me, since you are separated from It in My service. You give back to the truth what you have received from My Love. I could not have given you anything greater. Your gratitude matches by that, the grace I have given you, the greatness of the Gift I made to you.

"Console yourselves if I do not call upon you to pour out your blood like the martyrs, there is Mine to make up for it. Every time that you are prevented from drinking It, I'll regard it the same as if you had spilt yours, and Mine is far more precious."

So that is how we find the Eucharist, even during the deprivation of the Eucharist. From another view, who is able to separate us from Christ and His Church in Communion in approaching its altars by Faith, in a much more efficacious manner since it is spiritual and further from the senses. It is what I call communicating spiritually in uniting oneself with the faithful who are able to do it in different places on the earth.

You were familiar with this sort of Communion in the times when you were able to go to the Holy Table. You knew the advantages and the manner of it, so I'll not discuss it with you, but I'm going to show you what Holy Scripture and the annals of the Church offer in reflections on the deprivation of the Mass, and the necessity of a continual Sacrifice for the faithful in times of persecution, and that briefly.

Give particular attention, my children, to the principles I'm going to recall. They are for your edification.

Nothing happens without the will of God! Whether we have a worship, which allows us to assist at Mass, or that we be deprived of it, let us be worthy.

The worship, which we owe to Christ depends on the assistance which He gives us and the necessity we have of His Help. This worship outlines for us our duties as isolated faithful just as it outlined for us before, in the public exercise of our religion.

As children of God according to the witness of Sts. Peter and John, we participated in the priesthood of Jesus Christ to offer prayers and promises. If we are not entitled to sacrifice on visible altars, we are not without offering, since we can offer it in worship by our love in sacrificing Christ ourselves to His Father on the invisible altar of our hearts.

Faithful to this principle, we shall gather all the graces that we would have been able to gather had we been able to assist at the Holy Sacrifice of the Mass. Charity unites us to all the faithful of the Universe who offer this Divine Sacrifice, or who assist at it. If we lack a material altar and sensible Species, there are no longer any in Heaven where Jesus Christ is offered in the most perfect manner. Yes, my children, the faithful who are without priests, being themselves priests and kings, according to St. Peter, offer their Sacrifice without temple, without minister and without anything sensible.

It needs only Jesus Christ to offer it.

"For the sacrifice of the heart, where the victum must be consumed by the fire of love for the Holy Ghost, it requires to be united to Jesus Christ," said St. Clement of Alexandria, "by words, by deeds and by heart."

We are united to Him by words when they are true, by our actions when they are just, by our hearts when Charity inflames them. So, let us speak the truth, follow nothing but the truth, love nothing but the truth. Then we shall render to God the glory which is His due.

When we are true in our words, just in our actions, submit to God in our desires and thoughts, in speaking for Him alone, in praising Him for His gifts, in humiliating ourselves for oursins, we offer God an agreeable sacrifice, and which cannot be taken from us.

It remains for me to consider the Eucharist as a last Sacrament. You could be deprived of it at death so I must enlighten you and caution you against so terrible a deprivation.

Last Sacrament

God, Who loves and protects us, wishes to give us His Body at the approach of death, to take away our fear on this last journey. When you look to the future and see yourself on your own death-bed, without the last Sacrament, without Extreme Unction and without any help on the part of the ministers of the Lord, you see yourself abandoned in the most sad and terrible way.

Console yourselves, my children, in the trust you have in God.

This tender Father will pour on you His Graces, His blessings and His mercies, in these awful moments which you fear, in more abundance than if you were being assisted by His ministers of whom you have been deprived only because you wouldn't abandon Him, Himself.

The abandonment and forsakenness which we fear for ourselves, resembles that of the Saviour on the Cross when He said to His Father: "My God, My God, why have you forsaken me?" (Ps. 21.)

Ah! How constructive and consoling are these words! Your pains and abandonment lead you to your glorious destiny in ending your life like Jesus ended His. Jesus, in His sufferings, His abandonment and His death, was in most intimate union with His Father. In your pains and abandonment, be to Him likewise united, and let your last sigh be like His, that God's Will be done.

What I have said of the deprivation of the Last Sacrament at death, I will say of Extreme Unction. If I die in the hands of persons, who not only do not help me, but insult me, I shall be much happier that my death shall have more conformity with that of Jesus who was a spectacle of opprobrium to all the world. Crucified by the hand of His enemies, He was treated like a thief and died between two thieves. He was Wisdom itself and was taken for an idiot, He was the Truth, and He was taken for a cheat and deceiver. The Pharisees and Scribes triumphed over Him and in His Presence. They were finally stained with His Blood. Christ died in the most shameful infamy of torture and excruciating pains of the Cross. Christians, if your last moments and death are an occasion for your enemies to treat you with insults and disgrace, what were those of Jesus? I'm not sure the Angel who was sent to make up for the hard heartedness and callousness of men wasn't to teach us, that in similar circumstances, we receive the consolation of Heaven when that of men is missing. It was not without a special plan of God, that the Apostles who ought to have consoled Jesus, remained in a deep sleep.

So the faithful shouldn't be surprised to find himself without a priest in his last moments.

Jesus reproached His Apostles that they slept, but He didn't say that they left Him without consolation, to teach us, that if we go into the Garden of Olives, if we climb up to Calvary, if we die alone and without human help, God watches over us, consoles us, and for us that suffices.

Faithful, you are afraid of what follows the present time. Lift your eyes up to Jesus, keep them on Him, contemplate Him, He is your Model.

I can advise you nothing more.

After having contemplated on Him, would you still fear the deprivation of prayers and ceremonies of the Church which was established to sanctify and honour our last moments, our death and burial? Remember that the cause for which we suffer and die gives to this deprivation a new glory and gives to us the merit of the last bit of resemblance we can have to Jesus Christ. Providence has wished and permitted for our instruction that the Pharisees should put guards at the Sepulchre to guard the body of Jesus Crucified: it has even wished that after His Death, His Body should remain in the hands of His enemies, and that in order to teach us that however long the domination of our enemies might be, we must suffer it with patience and pray for them.

St. Ignatius the Martyr, who had so much ardour to be eaten by wild beasts, didn't he prefer to have them for a sepulchre than the most beautiful mausoleum? Even the first Christians who were delivered to the executioner, all the confessors and all the martyrs, never worried about their last moments nor their graves. None of them worried on what should become of their bodies.

Yes, my children, when one has trusted Jesus Christ all his life, he still trusts Him after his death. Jesus on the Cross and near to death, saw the woman who had followed Him from Galilee, who kept back, His Mother, Mary Magdalene and His Beloved Apostle were near the Cross in sorrow, silence and grief. There, my children, is the picture you shall see.

Most Christians feel sorry for those among the faithful who find themselves persecuted, but they keep themselves apart, while some like the Mother of Jesus go to the innocent which wickedness strikes down. I remark with St. Ambrose, that Jesus' Mother, who stayed at the foot of the Cross, knew that Her Son was dying for the redemption of mankind, and wishing to die with Him for the accomplishment of this great work, she didn't fear to annoy the Jews with Her Presence and desiring to die with Her Son.

When you see someone die all forsaken, my children, or by the sword of persecution, imitate the Mother of Jesus, and not the women who had followed Him from Galilee.

Be pierced with this truth: that the most glorious and salutary time to die is when virtue is strongest in our heart. One must never fear for a friend of Jesus Christ when he is suffering. Help him even by our looks and our tears.

That, my children, is what I believe I had to tell you. I believe it sufficient to answer your questions and calm your piety. I have put the principles without going into detail, which appears useless. Your reflections will certainly make up for it, and our conversations if Providence ever permits, shall be on what you have done and what will inspire you to new desires.

I must tell you, my children, not to worry at what you are witnessing. Faith is not allied to these terrors. The number of the elect was always small. Only fear that God doesn't reproach you for lack of Faith, and for not having been able to watch an hour with Him. I admit, however, that humility can grieve, but in so saying, I shall add that Faith must gladden, God does all. Bear this judgement, it is the only one worthy of you. The unbelievers themselves delivered this judgement when the Saviour was making miraculous cures. What He is doing now is far greater. In His mortal life He cured the body, but now, He cures souls and completes by trials the number of the elect.

Whatever are God's plans for us, let us adore the depth of His judgements and put all our confidence in Him. If He wishes to deliver us, the time is near. Everything turns against us, our friends oppress us, our relations treat us like strangers, the faithful who used to worship with us are turned away with a single look. They fear to say that not only like us, they are faithful to their country, submit to its laws, but unfaithful to God. They fear to stay without help alongside men, we are assured of God's help, who according to the King Prophet, will deliver the poor from the powerful and the weak who have no help.

The universe is the work of God. He reigns over it and every happening is according to the plans of His Providence. When we believe that desertion is going to be general, we forget that a little faith is enough to give faith to the family of Jesus, like a little leaven makes all the dough rise. These extraordinary events where the mobs wields the axe to undermine the work of God, serve marvellously to show His Omnipotence. In every country will be seen what the people of God saw. When the Lord was wanted by Gideon to show His Power against the Midianites, He had him send back most of his army. Three hundred men only and those without arms in order that it could be seen that the victory was God's. This small number of Gideon's soldiers, is the number of the faithful elect of that century. You have seen with the saddest astonishment, my children, that out of all those called, since all of France was Christian, the greater part, like in Gideon's army, remained weak, timid and fearing to lose their temporal interests. God sends them back, for use in His Justice, God only wants those who give themselves to Him entirely. Don't be surprised at the great number who quit. Truth wins, no matter how small the number of those who love and remain attached to Him. For my part, I have only one wish, the desire of St. Paul. As a child of the Church, as a soldier of Christ, I wish to die under His Standard.

If you have the works of St. Cyprian, read them, my dear children. One must go back to the first centuries of the Church to find worthy examples to serve as a model. It is in the Holy Books and in those of the first defenders of the Faith that one must form a precise idea of the object of martyrdom and of the confession of Jesus Christ. It is Truth and Justice. These are the august, eternal and unchangeable objects of the Faith which one must confess. It is the Gospel. For human instructions, however wise they may be, they are temporary and changeable. But the Gospel and the Law of God holds for Eternity. It is in thinking over this distinction that you will clearly see what is God's and what is Caesar's. As by the example of Christ you must render to one with respect, and to the other that which is his due.

Every Church and every century are in agreement that there is nothing more glorious and holy than to confess the Name of Jesus Christ, but remember, my dear children, that to confess It in a manner worthy of the crown which we desire, it is during the time one suffers most that one must have the greater holiness. I can find nothing more beautiful than the words of St. Cyprian when he praises all the Christian virtues in the confessors of Jesus Christ:

"You have always observed," he says to them, "the command of the Lord with a severity worthy of your firmness, you have conserved simplicity and innocence, charity and concord, modesty and humility, you have carried out your ministry with care and exactitude, you have been vigilant to help those who need help, to have compassion for the poor, of constance in defending the truth and discipline, in order that there be nothing wanting in these great examples of virtue which you have till now given, it is by your confession and generous sufferings that you highly animate your brethren to martyrdom and to show them the road."

I hope, children, although God doesn't call you to martyrdom nor to a distressing confession of His Name, to be able to speak to you one day as in the example of this illustrious martyr when he spoke to the confessors Celerius and Arele, and to praise in you your humility rather than your steadfastness and to glorify you more for your holiness than for your sufferings and wounds. In looking towards this happy moment, profit from my advice and sustain yourselves by my example, if necessary.

God watches over us, our hope is justified, it shows us either the persecution stops or the persecution will be our crown. In the alternative of one or the other, I see the accomplishment of our destiny.

Let God's Will be done, since in whatever manner He delivers us, His eternal Mercies pour onto us.

I end, my dear children, in embracing you and praying to God for you. Pray to Him for me and receive my paternal benediction as the pledge of my affection for you, as my faith and as my sincere resignation to have no other will but that of God."

Permanent Instruction Of The Alta Vendita

Printed in English in 1885 and discovered in Italian earlier and ordered published in 1859 by Pope Pius IX. Notice the Freemasons wanted to complete their plan within a century from 1859 (ie by 1959). Alta Vendita translated from the Italian means, "High Sale".

Ever since we have established ourselves as a body of action, and that order has commenced to reign in the bosom of the most distant lodge, as in that one nearest the center of action, there is one thought which has profoundly occupied the men who aspire to universal regeneration. That is the thought of the enfranchisement of Italy, from which must one day come the enfranchisement of the entire world, the fraternal republic, and the harmony of humanity. That thought has not yet been seized upon by our brethren beyond the Alps. They believe that revolutionary Italy can only conspire in the shade, deal some strokes of the poinard to sbirri and traitors, and tranquilly undergo the yoke of events which take place beyond the Alps for Italy, but without Italy. This error has been fatal to us on many occasions. It is not necessary to combat it with phrases which would be only to propagate it. It is necessary to kill it by facts. Thus, amidst the cares which have the privilege of agitating the minds of the most vigorous of our lodges, there is one which we ought never forget. The Papacy has at all times exercised a decisive action upon the affairs of Italy. By the hands, by the voices, by the pens, by the hearts of its innumerable bishops, priests, monks, nuns, and people in all latitudes, the Papacy finds devotedness without end ready for martyrdom, and that to enthusiasm. **Everywhere, whenever it pleases to call upon them, it has friends ready to die or lose all for its cause.** This is an immense leverage which the Popes alone have been able to appreciate to its full power, and as yet they have used it only to a certain extent. Today there is no question of reconstituting for ourselves that power, the prestige of which is for the moment weakened. **Our final end is that of Voltaire and of the French Revolution, the destruction for ever of Catholicism** and even of the Christian idea which, if left standing on the ruins of Rome, would be the resuscitation of Christianity later on. But to attain more certainly that result, and not prepare ourselves with gaiety of heart for reverses which adjourn indefinitely, or compromise for ages, the success of a good cause, we must not pay attention to those braggarts of Frenchmen, those cloudy Germans, those melancholy Englishmen, all of whom imagine they can kill Catholicism, now with an impure song, then with an illogical deduction. At another time, with a sarcasm smuggled in like the cottons of Great Britain. Catholicism has a life much more tenacious than that. It has seen the most implacable, the most terrible adversaries, and it has often had the malignant pleasure of throwing holy water on the tombs of the most enraged. Let us permit, then, our brethren of these countries to give themselves up to the sterile intemperance of their anti-Catholic zeal. Let them even mock at our Madonnas and our apparent devotion. With this passport we can conspire at our ease, and arrive little by little at the end we have in view. Now the Papacy has been for seventeen centuries inherent to the history of Italy. Italy cannot breathe or move without the permission of the Supreme Pastor. With him she has the hundred arms of Briareus, without him she is condemned to a pitiable impotence. She has nothing but divisions to foment, hatreds to break out, and hostilities to manifest themselves from the highest chain of the Alps to the lowest of the Appenines. We cannot desire such a state of things. It is necessary, then, to seek a remedy for that situation. The remedy is found. The Pope, whoever he may be, will never come to the secret societies. **It is for the secret societies to come first to the Church, in the resolve to conquer the two.** The work which we have undertaken is not the work of a day, nor of a month, nor of a year. It may last many years, a century perhaps, but in our ranks the soldier dies and the fight continues. We do not mean to win the Popes to our cause, to make them neophytes of our principles, and propagators of our ideas. That would be a ridiculous dream, no matter in what manner events may turn. Should cardinals or prelates, for example, enter, willingly or by surprise, in some manner, into a part of our secrets, it would be by no means a motive to desire their elevation to the See of Peter. That elevation would destroy us. Ambition alone would bring them to apostasy from us. The needs of power would force them to immolate us. That which we ought to demand, that which we should seek and expect, as the Jews expected the Messiah, is a Pope according to our wants. Alexander VI, with all his private crimes, would not suit us, for he never erred in religious matters. Clement XIV, on the contrary, would suit us from head to foot. Borgia was a libertine, a true sensualist of the eighteenth century strayed into the fifteenth. He has been anathematized, notwithstanding his vices, by all the voices of philosophy and incredulity, and he owes that anathema to the vigor with which he defended the Church. Ganganelli gave himself over, bound hand and foot, to the ministers of the Bourbons, who made him afraid, and to the incredulous who celebrated his tolerance, and Ganganelli is become a very great Pope. He is almost in the same condition that it is necessary for us to find another, if that be yet possible. With that we should march more surely to the attack upon the Church than with the pamphlets of our brethren in France, or even with the gold of England. Do you wish to know the reason? **It is because by that we should have no more need of the vinegar of Hannibal, no more need the powder of cannon, no more need even of our arms. We have the little finger of the successor of St. Peter engaged in the plot, and that little finger is of more value for our crusade than all the Innocents, the Urbans, and the St. Bernards of Christianity.** We do not doubt that we shall arrive at that supreme term of all our efforts, but when and how? The unknown does not yet manifest itself. Nevertheless, as nothing should separate us from the plan traced out. As, on the contrary, all things should tend to it, as if success were to crown the work scarcely sketched out tomorrow, we wish in this instruction which must rest a secret for the simple initiated, to give to those of the Supreme Lodge, councils with which they should enlighten the universality of the brethren, under the form of an instruction or memorandum. It is of special importance, and because of a discretion, the motives of which are transparent, never to permit it to be felt that these counsels are orders emanating from the Alta Vendita. The clergy is put too much in peril by it, that one can at the present hour permit oneself to play with it, as with one of these small affairs or of these little princes upon which one need but blow to cause them to disappear. Little can be done with those old cardinals or with those prelates, whose character is very decided. It is necessary to leave them as we find them, incorrigible, in the school of Consalvi, and draw from our magazines of popularity or unpopularity the arms which will render useful or ridiculous the power in their hands. A word which one can ably invent and which one has the art to spread amongst certain honourable chosen families by whose means it descends into the cafes, and from the cafes into the streets. A word can sometimes kill a man. If a prelate comes to Rome to exercise some public function from the depths of the provinces, know presently his character, his antecedents, his qualities, his defects above all things. If he is in advance, a declared enemy, an Albani, a Pallotta. a Bernetti, a Della Genga, a Riverola? Envelope him in all the snares which you can place beneath his feet. Create for him one of those reputations which will frighten little children and old women. Paint him cruel and sanguinary. Recount, regarding him, some traits of cruelty which can be easily engraved in the minds of the people. When foreign journals shall gather for us these recitals, which they will embellish in their turn, (inevitably because of their respect for truth) show, or rather cause to be shown, by some respectable fool those papers where the names and the excesses of the personages implicated are related. As France and England, so Italy will never be wanting in facile pens which know how to employ themselves in these lies so useful to the good cause. With a newspaper, the language of which they do not understand, but in which they will see the name of their delegate or judge, the people have no need of other proofs. They are in the infancy of liberalism. They believe in liberals, as, later on, they will believe in us, not knowing very well why. Crush the enemy whoever he may be. Crush the powerful by means of lies and calumnies, but especially crush him in the egg. **It is to the youth we must go. It is that which we must seduce. It is that which we must bring under the banner of the secret societies.** In order to advance by steps, calculated but sure, in that perilous way, two things are of the first necessity. You ought have the air of being simple as doves, but you must be prudent as the serpent. Your fathers, your children, your wives themselves, ought always be ignorant of the secret which you carry in your bosoms. If it pleases you, in order the better to deceive the inquisitorial eye, to go often to confession, you are, as by right authorized, to preserve the most absolute silence regarding these things. You know that the least revelation, that the slightest indication escaped from you in the tribunal of penance, or elsewhere, can bring on great calamities, and that the sentence of death is already pronounced upon the revealer, whether voluntary or involuntary. Now then, in order to secure to us a Pope in the manner required, it is necessary to fashion for that Pope a generation worthy of the reign of which we dream. Leave on one side old age and middle life, go to the youth, and, if possible, even to infancy. Never speak in their presence a word of impiety or impurity,

"Maxima debetur puero reverentia."[1] Never forget these words of the poet for they will preserve you from licenses which it is absolutely essential to guard against for the good of the cause. In order to reap profit at the home of each family, in order to give yourself the right of asylum at the domestic hearth, you ought to present yourself with all the appearance of a man grave and moral. Once your reputation is established in the colleges, in the gymnasiums, in the universities, and in the seminaries. Once that you shall have captivated the confidence of professors and students, so act that those who are principally engaged in the ecclesiastical state should love to seek your conversation. **Nourish their souls with the splendors of ancient Papal Rome.** There is always at the bottom of the Italian heart a regret for Republican Rome. Excite, enkindle those natures so full of warmth and of patriotic fire. Offer them at first, but always in secret, inoffensive books, poetry resplendent with national emphasis. Then little by little you will bring your disciples to the degree of cooking desired. When upon all the points of the ecclesiastical state at once, this daily work shall have spread our ideas as the light, then you will be able to appreciate the wisdom of the counsel in which we take the initiative. Events, which in our opinion, precipitate themselves too rapidly, go necessarily in a few months' time to bring on an intervention of Austria. There are fools who in the lightness of their hearts please themselves in casting others into the midst of perils, and meanwhile, there are fools who at a given hour drag in even wise men. The revolution which they meditate in Italy will only end in misfortunes and persecutions. Nothing is ripe, neither the men nor the things, and nothing shall be for a long time yet, but from these evils you can easily draw one new chord, and cause it to vibrate in the hearts of the young clergy. That is the hatred of the stranger. Cause the German to become ridiculous and odious even before his foreseen entry. With the idea of the Pontifical supremacy, mix always the old memories of the wars of the priesthood and the Empire. Awaken the smoldering passions of the Guelphs and the Ghibellines, and thus you will obtain for yourselves the reputation of good Catholics and pure patriots. That reputation will open the way for our doctrines to pass to the bosoms of the young clergy, and go even to the depths of convents. **In a few years the young clergy will have, by the force of events,**

---

[1]   "The greatest reverence owed to a child."

invaded all the functions. They will govern, administer, and judge. They will form the council of the Sovereign. **They will be called upon to choose the Pontiff who will reign** and that Pontiff, like the greater part of his contemporaries, will be necessarily imbued with the Italian and **humanitarian principles which we are about to put in circulation.** It is a little grain of mustard which we place in the earth, but the sun of justice will develop it even to be a great power, and you will see one day what a rich harvest that little seed will produce. In the way which we trace for our brethren there are found great obstacles to conquer, difficulties of more than one kind to surmount. They will be overcome by experience and by perspicacity, but the end is beautiful. What does it matter to put all the sails to the wind in order to attain it. **You wish to revolutionize Italy? Seek out the Pope of whom we give the portrait.** You wish to establish the reign of the elect upon the throne of the prostitute of Babylon? Let the clergy march under your banner in the belief always that they march under the banner of the Apostolic Keys. You wish to cause the last vestige of tyranny and of oppression to disappear? Lay your nets like Simon Barjona. Lay them in the depths of sacristies, seminaries, and convents, rather than in the depths of the sea, and if you will precipitate nothing you will give yourself a draught of fishes more miraculous than his. The fisher of fishes will become a fisher of men. You will bring yourselves as friends around the Apostolic Chair. You will have fished up a Revolution in Tiara and Cope, marching with Cross and banner. A Revolution which it will need but to be spurred on a little to put the four quarters of the world on fire. Let each act of your life tend then to discover the Philosopher's Stone. The alchemists of the middle ages lost their time and the gold of their dupes in the quest of this dream. **That of the secret societies will be accomplished for the most simple of reasons, because it is based on the passions of man.** Let us not be discouraged then by a check, a reverse, or a defeat. Let us prepare our arms in the silence of the lodges, dress our batteries, flatter all passions the most evil and the most generous, and all lead us to think that **our plans will succeed one day above even our most improbable calculations.**

A Catholic Utopia
By: Richard J. McHugh

Perhaps in no country not even Ireland are the beauty and sanctity of the Church seen to better advantage than in "The holy land Tyrol," as her children, with affectionate pride, designate her. For in no other land today are Church and State wedded in such happy union as in the Austro Hungarian Empire; and in the Empire itself, it may be safely said, no other State has won such renown for its sterling fealty to "Kaiser, Gott und Vaterland," as the mountain girdled home of the patriotic Hofer.

The loyalty of the Tyrolese peasant to the Church has become proverbial. His name, like that of his unfortunate Irish brother, is but a synonym of Catholic. His lively faith, untainted with the faintest suspicion of any modern heresy or fashionable "philosophy." The almost primitive simplicity of his manners. The unquestionable honesty of all his dealings. And the stainless purity of his morals, are the admiration and delight of all who behold them. While they serve not a little to prove to the Protestant world that cleanliness of heart and uprightness of character are not altogether incompatible with the teaching of the "Priests of Rome."

To the readers of the Record, and to those of them especially who live in parts, like America or Australia, where the Church, but yet in her lusty infancy is striving to beat down the barriers of bigotry, prejudice and intolerance, a short description of some of the religious customs of a land where the Church has flourished for fifteen centuries and is still loved, respected, and obeyed by her children, may not be devoid of interest. While the example of those privileged ones, who enjoy in full the blessings of our Holy Mother, may not be wanting, let us hope, in its salutary lesson to their less fortunate brethren in distant lands.

At the outset of my paper it may be appropriate to remark, that the people of the Tyrol always begin the day in that most excellent Christian manner by assisting at the Holy Sacrifice of the Mass. If they failed in this it would show them to be but very lax and careless Catholics indeed; for there is no village, howsoever small, in all the land, that cannot boast of at least one beautiful little chapel where the Saving Host is daily offered up to His Eternal Father. In the towns and cities the opportunities of hearing Mass, naturally, are ampler still, and as early as half past four in the morning the bells can be heard pealing through the misty air from dome and spire of church and convent, calling upon mankind to lift his waking thoughts to his Creator. From this hour, when even the birds are still sleeping in their nests, until 9 or 10 o'clock, on weekdays and Sundays alike, it is easy to find some church in which a Mass is being celebrated. And the throngs of faithful worshipers that fill the sacred temples at any time between these hours is a sight truly edifying.

Thrice a day, at the proper hours, the Angelus is rung, and as the first stroke of the bell is heard chiming in the air, recalling to the Christian soul the wonderful mystery of the Word made Flesh. The people, whether at home or in the streets, in the shop or marketplace, bow their heads and with reverent lips softly recite:

"The angel of the Lord declared unto Mary,
And she conceived of the Holy Ghost."

This time honored devotion, so simple and yet so sublime, did not fail to make a deep impression on the gentle heart of the American poet Longfellow as he witnessed it in Spain, and in his own beautiful way he thus describes it:

"Just as the evening twilight commences, the bell tolls to prayer. In a moment throughout the crowded city the hum of business is hushed, the thronged streets are still. The happy multitudes that crowd the public walks stand motionless. The angry dispute ceases. The laugh of merriment dies away. Life seems for a moment to be arrested in its career, and to stand still. The multitude uncover their heads, and, with the sign of the cross, whisper their evening prayer to the Virgin. Then the bells ring a merrier peal, the crowds move again in the streets, and the rush and turmoil of business recommence. I have always listened with feelings of solemn pleasure to the bell that sounded forth the Ave Maria. As it announced the close of day it seemed also to call the soul from its worldly occupations to repose and devotion. There is something beautiful in thus measuring the march of time. The hour, too, brings the heart into unison with the feelings and sentiments of devotion...It seems to me a beautiful and appropriate solemnity, that at the close of each daily epoch of life...The voice of the whole people and of the whole world should go up to Heaven in praise and supplication and thankfulness."

Every heart that is at all susceptible to the benign influence of religion must be thus impressed at the ringing of the Angelus bell, and gladly reecho the Protestant poet's words, for its mysterious effect is still the same, whether its chimes be heard along the vine clad slopes of Andalusia or amid the snow capped peaks of the Tyrolean Alps.

All through the Tyrol the tourist from Protestant lands is surprised to find the quiet country lanes, the rugged mountain passes, the very streets of the cities, adorned here and there with shrines of Our Lady, Crucifixes, and statues of saints to whom some special devotion is paid. Every bridge has its modest effigy of St. John Nepomuk, the heroic priest who braved the anger of the tyrant, Wenceslaus IV, of Bohemia, rather than violate the secrecy of the confessional, and received in consequence the crown of martyrdom by being thrown into the Moldau at the baffled king's command; and every house, almost, has a rude picture of St. Florian, the guardian of dwellings against fire, painted on its walls. "O God, through the intercession of thy servant Florian, protect us Thy children from the dangers of fire!" is an inscription often seen over the main entrances of private houses.

This pious custom of giving honor to the Most High, and seeking the patronage of His saints in a public manner, not long ago, as the readers of the Irish Ecclesiastical Record are aware, obtained throughout the greater part of Europe. But in many countries still claiming to be Christian the portraits of the saints have disappeared during the past years, and the Crucifix has gone down before the impious arm of the modern Iconoclast. In the Catholic Tyrol, however, the image of the Crucified Redeemer has not yet yielded its place to the effigy of Apollo, nor the statue of the Virginal Mother to the figure of Diana or the Cyprean Queen. Maria Theresien Strasse, in Innsbruck, has a beautiful specimen of Christian art, consisting of a magnificent shaft of highly polished granite, crowned with a marble statue of the "Immaculate Conception," and relieved at the base with life sized figures of Saints Joachim, Ann, Joseph and John. In passing these pious representations, the peasant respectfully bares his head and offers up a brief and silent prayer. Votive lamps burn continually before many shrines, and in harvest time the first two ears of corn plucked in the field are suspended from the arms of the nearest crucifix, in thanksgiving to the Son of God for having removed, by His sacred Passion and Death, the curse of old pronounced upon the earth and all its fruits, and for having restored the world to its primal grace and favor in the eyes of its Creator.

A mark of respect shown towards the Blessed Sacrament by the Tyrolean farmers is worthy of the imitation of all Catholic men. Not unmindful of the Prisoner of Love concealed within our tabernacles, they never fail to lift their hats in passing a church, and, indeed, not infrequently turn towards it and genuflect. When the priest carries the Viaticum through the streets the people on either side kneel, with uncovered heads, until he has passed; and in garrisoned towns whenever the Sacred Host is borne past the barracks, the guard is turned out to present arms to the King of Kings. Little acts of piety like these, after all, are what serve to keep the faith alive in our breasts in all its Apostolic fervor and secure to our souls many special graces from the Most High.

Early on summer mornings, when only the highest peaks are flushing with the rosy light of dawn, the village girls, pushing before them little carts, laden with vegetables and fresh laid eggs, come down from their mountain height to the market in the city. Having disposed of their tempting stock, and made whatever purchases are necessary for their humble life, they form into little companies and set out again for their aerial homes. And how, think you, do they while away the two or three weary hours of their difficult ascent up the rugged Alpine slopes? Not with idle gossiping or feminine small talk. Not in discussing the gorgeous feathers or shimmering silks exposed in the shop windows of the city. Ah, no! Foreign to the heart of the Tyrolese maiden are the thoughts of such frivolity. Strange as it may seem to the worldly minded, it is nevertheless an interesting fact, that the hours of their return are devoted to reciting in unison the Rosary of our Blessed Lady; and only that bright Angel who guards the Heavenly exchequer may say how many fragrant garlands of never fading flowers have thus been woven by those pure and simple village girls, and laid, a grateful offering, at the feet of the immaculate Queen of Virgins.

In the salutations that greet the pedestrian in his holiday rambles through a Tyrolese village there is something suggestive of the first days of Christianity. "Grüss' dich Gott!" (God salute you) and "Gelobt sei Jesus Christus!" (Praised be Jesus Christ) are among those most frequently heard. "Praised be Jesus Christ!" is certainly a beautiful and appropriate salutation for Christians, and when one hears it for the first time one seems to be suddenly transported back to the very days of the Apostles.

I was in the hospital not long ago in a neighboring city, and I remember what a sweet awakening it was, morning after morning, as the modest little sister entered with my breakfast, and called me back "from dreamland unto day," with her softly murmured ejaculation, "Gelobt sei Jesus Christus!" These were the first words that fell upon my ears at the opening of each new day, and the last I heard when day was over; for as the gentle sister smoothed my pillow for the night and sprinkled me with holywater, her parting words were ever, "Schlafen Sie wohl; Gelobt sei Jesus Christus!" Truly, a people in whose hearts and upon whose lips the blessed name of our divine Savior is thus with reverence ever found, may turn from this poor world when that Savior calls them, with souls strengthened with all the hope and love and confidence such faith as theirs must necessarily inspire.

An American friend of mine lately received an invitation to a Tyrolese wedding. As it is unique in its way and will serve as a further specimen of the deep piety that pervades these people, it may not be altogether inappropriate to give it insertion. It was printed on common paper and read as follows:

Praised Be Jesus Christ!

Esteemed and Beloved Friend, having entered, through God's will, into holy and honorable espousals with Maria G_____, I hereby humbly invite you to be present at our marriage, which will take place on the eighth day of the Spring month (i.e., March 8), in the most worthy House of God at V_____. A breakfast will be served at the house of our honored pastor, and a dinner at the inn of our excellent townsman, Joseph H_____. May everything tend to the greater honor of God and the holy Sacrament of Matrimony. Trusting you will honor us with your presence on this joyful occasion, and recommending you to the protection of God and the Blessed Virgin, I am, etc., etc., C. J.

Like unto this, methinks, might the invitation have been that was issued for the marriage feast given of old in the little village of Cana in Galilee, and which of all marriage feasts was blessed by Heaven. For, as we read, "the Mother of Jesus was there and Jesus was also invited and His disciples."

Briefly and at random I have touched upon a few pious customs that attract the attention of the stranger in this happy land. To describe in full the deep religious current that sends its purifying waters through the daily life of the Tyrolese. To speak of the thousand and one little acts of devotion that distinguish them in the field, at the fireside, or in the shop. To dwell upon the exterior pomp and interior fervor with which they hail the often recurring festivals of the Church, would require more space than I may ask of the Record in a single number. But I may say in conclusion that I never mingle with these simple hearted peasants or see them at their labors, their devotions, or their rustic merry makings, without thinking that in them is realized the fervent aspiration of the prayer.

Actiones nostras, quaesumus, Domine, aspirando praeveni et adjuvando prosequere; ut cuncta nostra oratio et operatio a te semper incipiat et per te coepta finiatur. (We beg Thee, O Lord, our prayers and our actions by Thy holy inspirations and carry them on by Thy Gracious assistance, so that every work of ours may Always begin with Thee, and through Thee come to completion. Amen.)

And with this sincere conviction I would give the Tyrol, before all other lands, the title of honor which I have taken as the subject of my paper: "A Catholic Utopia."

Richard J. McHugh

Lecture on the Great Apostasy given by Henry Edward Cardinal Manning

Before we enter upon the last subject which remains, let us take up the point at which we broke off in the last Lecture. It was this, that there are upon earth two great antagonists—on the one side, the spirit and the principle of evil; and on the other, the incarnate God manifested in His Church, but eminently in His Vicar, who is His representative, the depository of His prerogatives and therefore His special personal witness, speaking and ruling in His name. The office of the Vicar of Jesus Christ contains, in fullness, the Divine prerogatives of the Church: forasmuch as, being the special representative of the Divine Head, he bears all His communicable powers in the government of the Church on earth solely and alone. The other bishops and pastors, who are united with him, and act in subordination to him, cannot act without him; but he may act alone, possessing a plenitude of power in himself. And further, the endowments of the body are the prerogatives of the head and, therefore, the endowments which descend from the Divine Head of the Church upon the whole mystical body are centred in the head of that body upon earth; forasmuch as he stands in the place of the Incarnate Word as the minister and witness of the Kingdom of God among men. Now, it is against that person eminently and emphatically, as said before, that the spirit of evil and of falsehood direct its assault; for if the head of the body be smitten, the body itself must die. "Smite the shepherd, and the sheep shall be scattered," was the old guile of the evil one, who smote the Son of God that he might scatter the flock. But that craft has been once tried, and foiled for ever; for in the death which smote the Shepherd, the flock was redeemed: and though the shepherd who is constituted in the place of the Son be smitten, the flock can be scattered no more. Three hundred years the world strove to cut off the line of the Sovereign Pontiffs; but the flock was never scattered: and so it shall be to the end. It is, nevertheless, against the Church of God, and above all against its Head, that all the spirits of evil in all ages, and, above all, in the present, direct the shafts of their enmity. We see, therefore, what it is that hinders the manifestation, the supremacy, and the dominion of the spirit of evil and of disorder upon earth—namely, the constituted order of Christendom, the supernatural society of which the Catholic Church

39

has been the creator, the bond of union, and the principle of conservation; and the head of that Church, who is eminently the principle of order—the centre of the Christian society which binds the nations of the world in peace. Now the subject which remains to us is far more difficult. It reaches into the future, and deals with agencies so transcendent and mysterious, that all I shall venture to do will be to sketch in outline what the broad and luminous prophecies, especially of the book of Daniel and of the Apocalypse, set forth; without attempting to enter into minute details, which can only be interpreted by the event.

And further, as I said in the beginning, I shall not attempt anything except under the direct guidance of the theology of the Church, and of writers whose works have its approbation. As 1 have ventured hitherto nothing of my own, so until the end I shall pursue the same course.

What I have, then, to speak of is, the persecution of Antichrist, and finally his destruction.

First of all, let us begin with the twenty-fourth chapter of the holy Gospel according to St. Matthew, in which we read that our Divine Lord said when He beheld the buildings of the Temple, "There shall not be left here a stone upon a stone that shell not be destroyed." And His disciples, when He was in the Mount of Olives, Came to Him privately and said, Tell us what will be the sign of Thy coming, and of the consummation of the world." They understood that the destruction of thy Temple in Jerusalem and the end of the world should be part of one and the same action, and should take place at one and the same time. Now, as in nature we see mountains foreshortened one against another, so that the whole chain shares but one form, so in the events of prophecy, there are here two different events which appear but one the destruction of Jerusalem, and the end of the world. Our Divine Lord went on to tell them that there should come such a tribulation as had never yet been; and that unless those days were shortened, there should no flesh be saved; that for the sake of the elect those days should be shortened; that kingdom should rise against kingdom, and nation against nation, and there should be wars and pestliences and famines in divers places; that brethren should betray their brethren to death, (Mark 13) that they should be persecuted for His Name's sake, that all men should hate them, that they should be put to death, and that false Christs and false prophets should arise And should seduce many; that is, there should come false teachers, pretended Messias; and that in the midst of all these persecutions Himself would come to judgment—that, like as the lightning cometh out of the east, and appeareth even unto the west, so shall also the coming of the Son of Man be.

In this answer our Divine Lord spoke of two events—one, the destruction of Jerusalem, and the other, the end of the world. The one has been fulfilled, and the other is yet, to come. This chapter of St. Matthew will afford us a key to the interpretation of the Apocalypse. That book may be divided into four parts. The first part describes the Church on earth, under the seven Churches to which the messages were sent by our Divine Lord. They represent, as a constellation, the whole Church on earth. The second part relates to the destruction of Judaism, and the overthrow of the Jewish people. The third part relates to the persecution of the church by the pagan city of Rome, and to its overthrow: and the fourth and last part relates to the peace of the Church under the figure of the heavenly Jerusalem corning down from heaven and dwelling among men. Many interpreters, especially the early age, and also writers such as Bossuet and others of a later date, have supposed the prophecies of the Apocalypse, excepting only the last chapters, to be fulfilled by the events which took place in the first six centuries—that the overthrow of Jerusalem, the persecution of the Church, and the destruction of pagan Rome. But it is the nature of prophecy gradually to unfold itself. As I said of mountains foreshortened to our sight, when we wind about their base, they begin, as it were, to disentangle their outlines and to reveal themselves as many and distinct; so it is with the events of prophecy. The action of the world moves in cycles; that is, as the wise man says, "what hath been shall be," and "there is nothing new under the sun;" and that which we have seen in the beginning, prophecy declares shall be once more at the end of the world. In the four divisions of the Book Apocalypse, we have seen chief agents: the Church, the Jews, and persecuting power, which was pagan Rome. Now, these three at this moment exist upon earth. There is the Church of God still; there is the ancient people of God, the Jewish race, still preserved, as we have already seen, by a mysterious providence, for some future instrumentality; and there is, thirdly, the natural society of man

41

without God, which took the form of paganism of old, and will take the form of infidelity in the last days. These three are the ultimate agents in the history of the modern world: first, the natural society of mankind; next, the dispersion of the Jewish people; and, thirdly, the universal Church The two last are the only bodies which interpenetrate into all nations and have an unity distinct and independent of them. They have greater power than any nation, and are deadly and changeless antagonists. Now the Church has had to undergo already two persecutions, one from the hand of the Jews and one also from the hand of the pagans; so the writers of the early ages, the Fathers both of the East and of the West, foretold that, in the last age of the world, the Church will have to undergo third persecution, more bitter, more bloody, more searching, and more fiery than any it has undergone as yet, and that from the hands of an infidel world revolted from the Incarnate Word. And therefore the Book Apocalypse, like the prophecy of St. Matthew, reveals two events, or two actions. There is the event which is past, the type and the shadow of the event to come, and there is the event which is still future, at the end of the world; and all the persecutions that have ever been hitherto are no more than the forerunners and the types of the last persecution which shall be.

We have already seen the parallel of the two mysteries, the mystery of impiety and the mystery of godliness; and also the parallel of the two cities, the City of God and the city of this world. There remains another parallel which it is necessary that we should examine in order to make clear that which I shall have to say hereafter. We read in the Book Apocalypse of two women. There is a woman clothed with the sun, and there is a woman sitting upon a beast covered with the names of blasphemy. Now it is clear that these two women, like the two mysteries and the two cities, represent again two antagonist spirits, two antagonist principles. In the twelfth chapter of the Book Apocalypse we read of the woman "clothed with the sun," having " the moon under her feet, and on her head a crown of twelve stars. No Catholic will be at a loss for an interpretation of these words; and even Protestant interpreters, in order to avoid seeing the immaculate Mother of God in this woman clothed with the sun, tell us that it signifies the Church. In this they are perfectly right,—only they speak but half the truth. The woman typifies or symbolises the Church, for this reason, that the symbol of the Church is the Incarnation, the woman with the child; the symbol of the Incarnation is the Mother of God. On the other hand, we need not go far to find the interpretation of the woman who sits upon the beast having the names of blasphemy, for the last verse of the seventeenth chapter says "The woman which thou sawest is the great city which hath kingdom over the kings of the earth." It is quite clear, then, the there is an antagonism between these two women —the Church under the symbol of the Incarnation, and the great city, the city of Rome, with the seven hills, which has kingdom over the kings the earth.

Now let us keep clearly in mind this distinction because interpreters, heated by the spirit of controversy, have been pleased to confound these two things together, and to tell us that this woman seated on the beast is the Church of Rome. But the Church of Rome is the Church of God, or least a part of it, even in the mind of these interpreters. How, then, can these two, which so contrary the one to the other, mean the same thing? In truth, as it was with Elymas magician, who, for his perverseness, could not hold the sun for a season, so they who heat themselves in controversy lose their sense. In the splendor of this vision they cannot see the truth, and about to find the Church of God in that which the type of its antagonist; fulfilling again the end self-deceit, that when the truth is upon earth mistake a falsehood for the truth, as when the true Christ was come, they knew Him not, and called Him Antichrist. As it was with His Person, so it is with His Church.

With these preliminary distinctions, let us begin the last part of our subject. What I have to speak of is the persecution which Antichrist shall inflict upon the Church of God. We have already seen reason to believe that as our Divine Lord delivered Himself into the hands of sinners when His time was come, and no man could lay hand upon Him, until of His own free will He delivered Himself over to their power, so in like manner it shall be with that Church of which He said, "Upon this rock will I build my Church, and the gates of hell shall not prevail against it." As the wicked did not prevail against Him even when they bound Him with cords, dragged Him to the judgment, blindfolded His eyes, mocked Him as a false King, smote Him on the head as a false Prophet, led Him away, crucified Him, and in the mastery of their power seemed to have absolute dominion over Him, so that He lay ground down and almost annihilated under their feet; and as, at that very time when He was dead and buried out of their sight, He was conqueror over all, and rose again the third day, and ascended into heaven, and was crowned, glorified, and invested with His royalty, and reigns supreme, King of kings and Lord of lords,—even shall it be with His Church: though for a time persecuted, and, to the eyes of man, overthrown and trampled on, dethroned, despoiled, mocked, and crushed, yet in that high time of triumph the gate of hell shall not prevail. There is in store for the Church of God a resurrection and an ascension, a royalty and a dominion, a recompense of glory for all it has endured. Like Jesus, it needs must suffer on the way to its crown; yet crowned it shall be with Him eternally. Let no one, then, be scandalised if the prophecy speak of sufferings to come. We are fond of imagining triumphs and glories for the Church on earth,—that the Gospel is to be preached to all nations, and the world to be converted, and all enemies subdued, and I know not what,—until some ears are impatient of hearing that there is in store for the Church a time of terrible trial: and so we do as the Jews of old, who looked for a conqueror, a king, and for prosperity; and when their Messias came in humility and in passion, they did not know Him. So, I am afraid, many among us intoxicate their minds with the visions of success and victory, and cannot endure the thought that there is a time of persecution yet to come for the Church of God. Let us hear, therefore, the words of the prophet Daniel. Speaking of the person whom St. John calls the Antichrist, whom he calls the king that shall work according to his own will, the prophet Daniel says, "He shall speak words against the High One,"—that is, the Almighty God,—"and shall crush the faints of the Most High." Again he says, "It"—that is, the power of this king—"was magnified even unto the strength of heaven: and it threw down of the strength, and of the stars and trod upon them. And it was magnified even to the prince of the strength: and it took away from him the continual sacrifice, and cast down the place of his sanctuary." Further, he says, "The victim and the sacrifice shall fail, and there shall be in the temple the abomination of desolation." These three passages are taken from the seventh, and the eighth, and the ninth chapters of Daniel. I might add more, but they are enough, for in the Book Apocalypse (12:7) we find a key to these words. St. John, evidently referring to the Book of Daniel, writes of the beast, that is, the persecuting power which shall reign on the earth by might, "It was given unto him to make war with the saints and to

44

overcome them." Now here we have four distinct prophecies of a persecution which shall be inflicted by this antichristian power upon the Church of God. I will therefore point out as briefly as I can what appears in the events now around us to be leading on to this result.

1. The first sign or mark of this coming persecution is an indifference to truth. Just as there is dead calm before a whirlwind, and as the waters over a great fall run like glass, so before an outbreak there is a time of tranquillity. The first sign is indifference. The sign that portends more surely than any other the outbreak of a future persecution is a sort of scornful indifference to truth or falsehood. Ancient Rome in its might and power adopted every false religion from all its conquered nations, and gave to each of them a temple within its walls. It was sovereignly and contemptuously indifferent to all the superstitions of the earth. It encouraged them; for each nation had its own proper superstition, and that proper superstition was a mode of tranquillising, of governing, and of maintaining in subjection, the people who were indulged by building a temple within its gates. In like manner we see the nations of the Christian world at this moment gradually adopting every form of religious contradiction—that is, giving it full scope, and, as it is called, perfect toleration; not recognising any distinctions of truth or falsehood between one religion or another, but leaving all forms of religion to work their own way. I am not saying a word against this system if it be inevitable. It is the only system whereby freedom of conscience is now maintained. I only say, miserable is the state of the world in which ten thousand poisons grow round one truth; miserable is the state of any country where truth is only tolerated. This is a state of great spiritual and intellectual danger; and yet it seems there is no alternative but that the civil governors leave perfect freedom of conscience, and therefore maintain themselves in a state of perfect indifference.

Let us see the result. First of all, the divine voice of the Church of God is thereby entirely ignored. They see no distinction between a doctrine of faith and a human opinion. Both are allowed to have free way. There are mixed together doctrines of faith with every form of heresy, until, as in England, we have all conceivable forms of belief, from the Council of Trent in all its rigour and in all its perfection, on the one hand, to the *Catechism of Positive Religion* on the other. We have every form of opinion started, and freely allowed, from the two extremes; the one of which is the worship of God in Unity and Trinity, incarnate for us; and the other, the denial of God, and the worship of humanity. Next, denying and ignoring of course the divine voice of the Church, the civil governor must ignore the divine unity of the Church, and admit every form of separation, or system, or division all mingled together; so that the people are crumbled into religious sects and religious divisions, and the law of unity is entirely lost. Then, again, all positive truth, as such, is despised; and it is despised, because who shall say who is right and who is wrong, if there be no Divine teacher? If there be no Divine judge, who shall say what is into and what is false between conflicting religious opinions? A state that has separated itself from the unity of the Church, and thereby has lost the guidance of the Divine teacher, is unable to determine by any of its tribunals, civil or ecclesiastical. as it may continue to call them, what is true and what is false in a controverted question of religion; and then, as we know, there grows up an intense hatred of what is called dogmatism, that is, of any positive truth, any thing definite, any thing final, any thing which has precise limits, any form of belief which is expressed in particular definitions—all this is utterly distasteful to men who on principle encourage all forms of religious opinion. In fact, we are coming to the state of Festus, who, when he heard that the Jews had an accusation against St. Paul, reported that he could find "no question which seemed ill" to him, because they were questions superstition, and "about one Jesus deceased, whom Paul affirmed to be alive." (Acts xx. 18, 19.) Now this is just the state of indifference to which the civil governors of the world are gradually reducing themselves, and the government they administer, and the people they govern.

2. The next step is, then, the persecution of the truth. When Rome in ancient days legalised every idolatry throughout the whole of the Roman Empire, there was one religion which was called a religio illicita, an unlawful religion, and there was one society which was called a societas illicita, or an unlawful society. They might worship the twelve gods of Egypt, or Jupiter Capitolinus, or Dea Roma; but they might not worship the God of heaven, they might not worship God, revealed in His Son. They did not believe in the Incarnation; and that one religion which was alone true was the only religion that was not tolerated. There were the priests of Jupiter, of Cybele, of Fortune, and of Vesta; there were all manner of sacred confraternities, and orders,

and societies, and I know not what; but there was one society which was not permitted to exist, and that was the Church of the living God. In the midst of this universal toleration, there was one exception made with the most peremptory exactness, to exclude the truth and the Church of God from the world. Now this is what must again inevitably come to pass, because the Church of God is inflexible in the mission committed to it. The Catholic Church will never compromise a doctrine; it will never allow two doctrines to be taught within its pale; it will never obey the civil governor pronouncing judgment in matters that are spiritual. The Catholic Church is bound by the Divine law to suffer martyrdom rather than compromise a doctrine, or obey the law of the civil governor which violates the conscience; and more than this, it is not only bound to offer a passive disobedience, which may be done in a corner, and therefore not detected, and because not detected not punished; but the Catholic Church cannot be silent; it cannot hold its peace; it cannot cease to preach the doctrines of Revelation, not only of the Trinity and of the Incarnation, but likewise of the Seven Sacraments, and of the infallibility of the Church of God, and of the necessity of unity, and of the sovereignty, both spiritual and temporal, of the Holy See; and because it will not be silent, and cannot compromise, and will not obey in matters that are of its own Divine prerogative, therefore it stands alone in the world; for there is not another Church so called, nor any community professing to be a Church, which does not submit, or obey, or hold its peace, when the civil governors of the world command. It is not ten years since we heard of a decision on the matter of baptism, involving the doctrine of original sin on the one hand, end the doctrine of preventing grace on the other; and because a civil judge pronounced that it was lawful in the Established Church of England for men without punishment to teach two contradictory doctrines, bishops, priests, and people were content that it should be so: or, at least, they said, "We cannot do otherwise; the civil power will allow men to preach both: what can we do? We are persecuted, and therefore we hold our peace; we go on ministering under a civil law which compels us to endure that the man who preaches before us in the morning, or the man who shall preach after us in the afternoon, may preach a doctrine in diametrical contradiction to that which we know to be the revealed doctrine of God; and because the civil governors have determined it so, we are not responsible, and the Established Church is not responsible, because it is persecuted." Now this is the characteristic difference between a human system established by the civil law and the Church of God. Would it be permitted in the Church which is Catholic and Roman, that I should now deny that every child baptised receives the infusion of regenerating grace? What would become of me by tomorrow morning? You know perfectly well that if I were to depart one jot or one tittle from the Hay Catholic faith, delivered by the Divine voice of the Church of God, I should be immediately suspended. and no civil governor, or power in the world, could restore me to the exercise of my faculties; no civil judge or potentate on earth could restore me to the administration of the Sacraments, until the spiritual authority of the Church permitted me to do so.

This, then, is the characteristic difference, which must one day bring down upon the Church, in all countries where this spirit of indifference has established itself, a persecution of the civil power. And for a further reason, because the difference between the Catholic Church and every other society is this other societies are of voluntary formation; that is, people unite themselves to a particular body, and, they do not like it on better knowledge, they go their way: they become Baptists, or Anabaptists, or Episcopalians, or Unitarians, or Presbyterians, until they find something which they do not like in these stems; and then they go their way, and either unite themselves to some other body or remain unattached; because the societies have no claim to govern the will,—all that they profess to do is to teach. They are like the ancient school, and their teaching is a kind of Christian philosophy. They put their doctrines before those who are willing to listen, and if they listen, and, by good fortune agree with them, they remain with them: if not. they go their way. But where is the government over the will? Can they say, "In the name of God, and under pain of mortal sin, you must believe that God was incarnate, and that our incarnate Lord offers Himself in sacrifice upon the altar, that the Sacraments instituted by the Son of God are seven, and that they all convey the grace of the Holy Ghost" Unless they have an authority over the will as well as over the intelligence, they are only a school, and not a kingdom. Now this is a character entirely wanting in every society that cannot claim to govern in the name of our Divine Lord, and with a Divine voice and therefore the Church of God differs from every other society in this particular, that it is not only a communion of people who voluntarily unite together, but that it is a kingdom, It has a legislature; the line of its councils for eighteen hundred years have deliberated, and decreed with all the solemnity and the majesty of an imperial parliament. It has executive which carries out and enforces the decree of those councils with all the calmness and all the peremptory decision of an imperial will. The Church of God, therefore, is an empire within an empire; and the governors and princes of this world are jealous of it for that very reason. They say, "Nolumus hunc regnare super nos"—"we will not have this man to reign over us" It is precisely because the Son of God, when He came, established a kingdom upon earth, that therefore, in every land, in even nation, the Catholic Church governs with the authority of the universal Church of God. For instance, in England, the little and despised flock of Catholics united together under a hierarchy of ten years old, resting upon the Holy See as its centre, speaks and governs with a sovereignty derived from the whole Church of God. Therefore it is that ten years back the atmosphere was rent and tormented by the uproar of "Papal aggression." The natural instinct of the civil rulers knew that it was not a mere Christian philosophy wafted from foreign lands, but a government, a power, and a sovereignty. For this reason also, the extreme liberal school—those who claim toleration for every form of opinion, and who teach that the office of the civil governor is never to enter into controversies of religion, but that all men should be left free in their belief, and the conscience of all men be at liberty before God—even they make one exception, and, in the strangest contradiction to all their principles, or, at least, their professions. maintain that as the Catholic Church is not only a form of doctrine, but also a power or government, it must be excepted from the general toleration. And this is precisely the point of future collision. It is the very reason why the Archbishops of Cologne, Turin, Cagliari, and the like, went the other day into exile; why nineteen Sees are, at this moment, vacant in Sardinia. Why, in Italy, Bishops are, at this day, cast out from their Episcopal thrones: it is for this reason that in this land the Protestant religion is established instead of Catholic truth, and that thrones once filled by the Bishops of the universal Church are now occupied by those whom the royalties of England, and not the royalties of the Vicar of Jesus Christ, have chosen and set up. It is the same old contest, old as

49

Christianity itself, which has been from the beginning, first with pagan, and then with heretic, and then with schismatic, and then with infidel, and will continue to the end. The day is not far off, when the nations of the world, now so calm and peaceful in the stillness of their universal indifference, may easily be roused, and penal laws once more may be found in their Statute-books.

3. This leads on plainly to the marks which the prophet gives of the persecution of the last days. Now there are three things which he has recorded. In the foresight of prophecy he saw and noted these three signs. The first, that the continual sacrifice shall be taken away; the next, that the sanctuary shall be occupied by the abomination which maketh desolate; the third, that "the strength" and "the stars," as he described it: shall be cast down: and these are the only three I will notice.

Now, first of all what is this "taking away of the continual sacrifice"?

It was taken away in type at the destruction of Jerusalem. The sacrifice of the Temple, that is, of the lamb, morning and evening, in the Temple of God, was entirely abolished with the destruction of the Temple itself. Now the Prophet Malachias says: "From the rising of the sun even to the going down, any name is great among the Gentiles; and in every place there is sacrifice, and there is offered to my name a clean oblation." This passage of the prophet has been interpreted by the Fathers of the Church. beginning with St. Irenaeus, St. Justin Martyr, and I know not how many besides, to be the sacrifice of the Holy Eucharist, the true Paschal lamb which came in the place of the type— namely, the sacrifice of Jesus Himself on Calvary renewed perpetually and continued for ever in the sacrifice on the altar. Now has that continual sacrifice been taken away? That which was typical of it in old days has been already taken away. But has the reality been taken away? The holy Fathers who have written upon the subject of Antichrist, and of these prophecies of Daniel, without a single exception, as far as I know, and they are the Fathers both of the East and of the West, the Greek and the Latin Church—all of them unanimously,—say that in the latter end of the world, during the reign of Antichrist, the holy sacrifice of the altar will cease. In the work on the end of the world, ascribed to St. Hippolytus, after a long description of the afflictions of the last days, we read as follows: "The Churches shall lament with a great lamentation, for there shall be offered no more oblation, nor incense, nor worship acceptable to God. The sacred buildings of the churches shall be as hovels; and the precious body and blood of Christ shall not be manifest in those days; the Liturgy shall be extinct; the chanting of psalms shall cease; the reading of Holy Scripture shall be heard no more. But there shall be upon men darkness, and mourning upon mourning, and woe upon woe." Then, the Church shall be scattered, driven into the wilderness, and shall be for a time, as it was in the beginning, invisible, hidden in catacombs, in dens, in mountains, in lurking-places; for a time it shall be swept, as it were, from the face of the earth. Such is the universal testimony of the Fathers of the early centuries. Has there ever come to pass anything which may be called an installment or a forerunner of such an event as this? Look into the East. Mahometan superstition, which arose in Arabia, swept over Palestine and Asia Minor, the Seven Churches, and Egypt, the north of Africa—the home of St. Augustine, St. Cyprian, St. Optatus—and finally penetrated into Constantinople, soon it became dominant, has in every place persecuted and suppressed the worship and sacrifices of Jesus Christ. The Mahometan superstition at moment holds for its mosques a multitude of Christian churches, in which the continual sacrifice is already taken away, and the altar utterly destroyed. In Alexandria and in Constantinople there stand churches built for Christian worship, into which the foot of no Christian has ever entered since the continual sacrifice has been swept away. Surely in this we see, in part at least, the fulfilment of this prophecy; so much so, that many interpreters will have it that Mahomet is the Antichrist, and that none other is to come. No doubt he was one of the many forerunners and types of the Antichrist that shall be. Now let us look into the Western world: has the continual sacrifice been taken away in any other land? —for instance, in all those churches of Protestant Germany which were once Catholic, where the holy sacrifice of the Mass was daily offered! — throughout Norway, and Sweden, and Denmark, and one half of Switzerland, where there are a multitude of ancient Catholic churches — through England, in the cathedrals and the parish churches of this land, which were built simply as shrines of Jesus incarnate in the Holy Eucharist, as sanctuaries raised for the offering of the Holy Sacrifice? What is the characteristic mark of the Reformation, but the rejection of the Mass, and all that belongs to it, as declared in the Thirty-nine Articles of the

Church of England to be blasphemous fables and dangerous deceits? The suppression of the continual sacrifice is, above all, the mark and characteristic of the Protestant Reformation. We find, then, that this prophecy of Daniel has already its fulfilment both the East and West,— in the two wings, as it were while in the heart of Christendom the Holy Sacrifice is offered still. What is the great flood of in infinitely infidelity, revolution, and anarchy, which is now sapping the foundations of Christian society, not only in France, but in Italy, and encompassing Rome, the centre and sanctuary of the Catholic Church, but the abomination which desolates the sanctuary, and takes away the continual sacrifice? The secret societies have long ago undermined and honeycombed the Christian society of Europe, and are at this moment struggling onward toward, Rome, the centre of all Christian order in the world. The fulfilment of the prophecy is yet to come; and that which we have seen in the two wings, we shall see also in the centre; and that great army of the Church of God will, for a time, be scattered. It will seem, for a while, to be defeated, and the power of the enemies of the faith for a time to prevail. The continual sacrifice will be taken away, and the sanctuary will be cast down. What can be more literally the abomination which makes desolate than the heresy which has removed the presence of the living God from the altar? If you would understand this prophecy of desolation, enter into a church: which was once Catholic, where now is no sign of life; it stands empty, untenanted, without altar, without tabernacle, without the presence of Jesus. And that which has already come to pass in the East and in the West is extending itself throughout the centre of the Catholic unity.

The Protestant spirit of England, and the schismatical spirit even of countries Catholic in name. is at this moment urging on the great anticatholic movement of Italy- Hostility to the Holy See is the true and governing motive. And thus we come to the third mark, the casting down of "the Prince of Strength;" that is, the Divine authority of the Church, and especially of him in whose person it is embodied, the Vicar of Jesus Christ. God has invested him with sovereignty, and given to him a home and a patrimony en earth. The world is in arms to depose him, and to leave him no place to lay his head- Rome and the Roman States are the inheritance of the Incarnation. The world is resolved to drive the Incarnation off the earth. It will not suffer it to possess so much as to set the sole of its foot upon. This is the true interpretation of the anticatholic movement of Italy England: "Tolle hunc de terra." The dethronement of the Vicar of Christ is the dethronement of the hierarchy of the universal Church, and the public rejection of the Presence and Reign of Jesus.

4. Nor, if I am obliged to enter somewhat into the future, I shall confine myself to tracing out very general outline. The direct tendency of all the events we see at this moment is clearly this, to overthrow Catholic worship throughout the world. Already we see that every Government in Europe is excluding religion from its public acts. The civil powers are desecrating themselves: government is without religion; and if government be without religion, education must be without religion. We see it already in Germany and in France. It has been again and again attempted in England. The result of this can be nothing but the re-establishment of mere natural society; that is to say, the governments and the powers of the world, which for a time were subdued by the Church of God to a belief in Christianity, to obedience to the laws of God, and to the unity of the Church, having revolted from it and desecrated themselves, hare relapsed into their natural state

The Prophet Daniel, in the twelfth chapter, says that in the time of the end "many shall be chosen and made white, and shall be tried as fire; and the wicked shall deal wickedly, and none of the wicked shall understand, but the learned shall understand;" that is, many who have known the faith shall abandon it, by apostasy. "Some of the learned shall fall;" (Daniel 11:33) that is, they shall fall from their fidelity to God. And how shall this come to pass? Firstly by fear, partly by deception, partly by cowardice partly because they cannot stand for unpopular truth in the face of popular falsehood; partly because the overruling contemptuous public opinion, as in such country as this, and in France, so subdues and frightens Catholics, that they dare not avow their principles, and, at last, dare not hold them. They become admirers and worshipers of the material prosperity of Protestant countries. They see the commerce, the manufacture, the agriculture, the capital, the practical science, the irresistible armies, and the fleets that cover the sea, and they come flocking to adore, and say, "Nothing is so great as this great country of Protestant England." And so they give up their faith, and become materialists, seeking for the wealth and power of this world, dazzled and overpowered by the greatness of a country which has cast off its fidelity to the Church.

53

5. Now the last result of all this will be a persecution, which I will not attempt to describe. It is enough to remind you of the words of our Divine Master: "Brother shall betray brother to death:" it shall be a persecution in which no man shall spare his neighbour, in which the powers of the world will wreak upon the Church of God such a revenge as the world before has never known. The Word of God tells us that towards the end of time the power of this world will became so irresistible and so triumphant that the Church of God will sink underneath its hand — that the Church of God will receive no more help from emperors, or kings, or princes, or legislatures, or nations, or peoples, to make resistance against the power and the might of its antagonist It will be deprived of protection. It will be weakened, baffled, and prostrate, and will lie bleeding at the feet of the powers of this world. Does this seem incredible? What, then, do we see at this moment? Look at the Catholic and Roman Church throughout the world. When was it ever more like its Divine Head in the hour when He was bound hand and foot by those who betrayed Him? Look at the Catholic Church, still independent, faithful to its Divine trust, and yet cast off by the nations of the world; at the Holy Father, the Vicar of our Divine Lord, at this moment mocked, scorned, despised, betrayed, abandoned, robbed of his own, and even those that would defend him murdered. When, I ask, was the Church of God ever in a weaker condition, in a feebler state in the eyes of men, and in this natural order, than it is now? And from whence, I ask, is deliverance to come? Is there on earth any power to intervene? Is there any king, prince, or potentate, that has the power to interpose either his will or his sword for the protection of the Church? Not one; and it is foretold it should be so. Neither need we desire it, for the will of God seems to be otherwise. But there is One Power which will destroy all antagonists; there is One Person who will break down and smite small as the dust of the summer threshing-floor all the enemies of the Church, for it is He who will consume His enemies "with the Spirit of His mouth," and destroy them "with the brightness of His coming." It seems as if the Son of God were jealous lest any one should vindicate His authority. He has claimed the battle to Himself; He has taken up the gage which has been cast down against Him; and prophecy is plain and explicit that the last overthrow of evil will be His; that it will be wrought by no man, but by the Son of God; that all the nations of the world may know that He, and He alone,

is King, and that He, and He alone, is God. We read in the Book Apocalypse of the city of Rome, that she said in the pride of her heart, "I sit as a queen, and am no widow, and sorrow I shall not see. Therefore shall her plagues come in one day, death, and mourning, and famine, and she shall be burned with the fire, because God is strong who shall judge her." Some of the greatest writers of the Church tell us that in all probability, in the last overthrow of the enemies of God, the city of Rome itself will he destroyed; it will be a second time punished by Almighty God, as it was in the beginning. There was never destruction upon earth comparable to the overthrow of Rome in ancient days. St. Gregory the Great, writing of it, says, "Rome a little while ago was seen to be the mistress of the world; what she now is we behold. Crushed by manifold and boundless miseries, by the desolation of her inhabitants, the inroads of enemies, the frequency of destruction, we set fulfilled in her the words of the Prophet against the city. Where is the senate; where now is the people? The bones are decayed, and the flesh is consumed. All the pomp of worldly greatness in her is extinguished. Her whole structure is dissolved. And we, the few who remain, are day by day harassed by the sword and by innumerable tribulations. Rome is empty and burning; ... her people have failed, and even her walls are falling ... Where now are they who once exulted in her glory? Where is their pomp; where their pride; where their constant and immoderate rejoicing?" There never was a ruin like to the overthrow of the great City of the Seven Hills, when the words of the prophecy were fulfilled: "Babylon is fallen"—like "a great millstone cast into the sea"

The writers of the Church tell us that in the latter days the city of Rome will probably become apostate from the Church and Vicar of Jesus Christ; and that Rome will again be punished, for he will depart from it; and the judgment of God will fall on the place from which he once reigned over the nations of the world. For what is it that makes Rome sacred, but the presence of the Vicar of Jesus Christ? What has it that should be dear in the sight of God, save only the presence of the Vicar of His Son? Let the Church of Christ depart from Rome, and Rome will be no more in the eye of God than Jerusalem of old. Jerusalem, the Holy City, chosen by God, was cast down and consumed by fire, because it crucified the Lord of Glory; and the city of Rome, which has been the seat of the Vicar of Jesus Christ for eighteen hundred years, if it become apostate, like Jerusalem of old, will suffer a like condemnation. And, therefore, the writers of the Church tell us that the city of Rome has no prerogative except only that the Vicar of Christ is there; and if it become unfaithful, the same judgments which fell on Jerusalem, hallowed though it was by the presence of the Son of God, of the Master, and not the disciple only, shall fall likewise upon Rome.

The apostasy of the city of Rome from the Vicar of Christ, and its destruction by Antichrist, may be thoughts so new to many Catholics, that I think it well to recite the text of theologians in the greatest repute. First, Malvenda, who writes expressly on the subject, states as the opinion of Ribera, Gaspar Melus, Viegas, Suarez, Bellarmine and Bosius, that Rome shall apostatise from the faith and drive away the Vicar of Christ, and return to its ancient paganism. Malvenda's words are: "Rome itself in the last times of the world will return to its ancient idolatry, power, and imperial greatness. It will cast out its Pontiff, altogether apostatise from the Christian faith, terribly persecute the Church, shed the blood of martyrs more cruelly than ever, and will recover its former state of abundant wealth, or even greater than it had under its first rulers."

Lessius says: "In the time of Antichrist, Rome shall be destroyed, as we see openly from the thirteenth chapter of the Apocalypse;" and again: "The woman whom thou sawest is the great city, which hath kingdom over the kings of the earth, in which is signified Rome in its impiety, such as it "as in time of St. John, and shall be again at the end of the world." And Bellarmine "In the time of Antichrist, Rome shall be desolated and burnt, as ye learn from the sixteenth verse of the seventeenth chapter of the Apocalypse." On which words the Jesuit Erbermann comments as follows: "We all confess with Bellarmine that the Roman people, a little before the end of the world, will return to Paganism, and drive out the Roman Pontiff."

Viegas, on the eighteenth chapter of the Apocalypse, says: "Rome, in the last age of the world, after it has apostatised from the faith, will attain to great power and splendour of wealth, and its sway will he widely spread throughout the world, and flourish greatly. Living in luxury and the abundance of all things, it will worship idols, and be steeped in all kinds of superstition, and will pay honour to false gods. And because of the vast effusion of the blood of martyrs which war shed under the emperors, God will most severely and justly avenge them, and it shell be utterly destroyed, and burned y a most terrible and afflicting conflagration."

Finally, Cornelius A. Lapide sums up what may be said to be the common interpretation of theologians. Commenting on the same eighteenth chapter of the Apocalypse, he says: "These things are to be understood of the city of Rome, not that which is, nor that which was, but that which shall ho at the end of the world. For then the city of Rome will return to its former glory, and likewise its idolatry and other sins, and shall be such as it was in the time of St. John, under Nero, Domitian, Decius, etc. For from Christian it shall again become heathen. It shall cast out the Christian Pontiff, and the faithful who adhere to him. It shall persecute and slay them. It shall rival the persecutions of the heathen emperors against the Christians. . . . . For so we see Jerusalem was first heathen under the Canaanite; secondly, faithful under the Jews; thirdly, Christian under the Apostles; fourthly, heathen again under the Romans; fifthly, Saracen under the Turks."

Such they believe will be the history of Rome: pagan under the emperors, Christian under the Apostles, faithful under the Pontiffs, apostate under the Revolution, and pagan under Antichrist. Only Jerusalem could sin so formally and fall so low; for only Jerusalem has been so chosen, illumined, and consecrated. And as no people were ever so intense, in their persecutions of Jesus as the Jews, so I fear will none ever be more relentless against the fair than the Romans.

Now I have not attempted to point out what shall be the future events except in outline, and I have never ventured to designate who shall be the person who shall accomplish them. Of this I know nothing; but I am enabled with the most perfect certainty, from the Word of God, and from the interpretations of the Church, to point out the great principles which are in conflict on either side I began by showing you that the Antichrist, and the antichristian movement, has these marks: first, schism from the Church of God; secondly, denial of its Divine and infallible voice; and thirdly, denial of the Incarnation. It is, therefore, the direct and mortal enemy of the One Holy Catholic and Roman Church—the unity from which all schism is made; the sole organ of the Divine voice of the Spirit of God; the shrine and sanctuary of the Incarnation and of the continual sacrifice.

And now to make an end. Men have need to look to their principles. They have to make a choice between two things, between faith in a teacher speaking with an infallible voice, governing the unity which now, as in the beginning, knits together the nations of the world, or the spirit of fragmentary Christianity, which is the source of disorder and ends in unbelief. Hero is the simple choice t which we arc all brought; and between them we must make up our minds.

The events of every day are carrying men further and further in the career on which they have entered. Every day men are becoming more and more divided. These are times of sifting. Our Divine Lord is standing in the Church: "His fan is in, His hand, and He will thoroughly cleanse His and He will gather the grain into His barn, and will burn up the chaff with unquenchable fire It is a time of trial, when "some of the learned shall fall," and those only shall be saved who is steadfast to the end. The two great antagonists are gathering their forces for the last conflict;—it may not be in our day, it may not be in the time of the, who come after us; but one thing is certain, that we are as much put on our trial now as they will he who live in the time when it shall come to pass. For as surely as the Son of God reigns on high, and will reign "until He has put all His enemies under His feet," so surely every one that lifts a heel or directs a weapon against His faith, His Church, or His Vicar car upon earth, will share the judgment which is laid up fur the Antichrist whom he serves.

THE END.

The Jewish Peril and the Catholic Church

The Catholic Gazette February 1936

Editorial note

That there has been and still is a Jewish problem, no one can deny. Since the rejection of Israel, 1,900 years ago, the Jews have scattered in every direction and in spite of difficulties and even persecution, they have established themselves as a power in nearly every nation of Europe. Jacobs in his <u>Jewish Contributions to Civilization</u>, glories in the fact that without detriment to their own racial unity and international character, the Jews have been able to spread their doctrines and increase their political, social and economic influence among the nations.

In view of this Jewish problem, which affects the Catholic church in a special way, we publish the following amazing extracts from a number of speeches recently made under the auspices of a Jewish society in Paris. The name of our informant must remain concealed. He is personally known to us but by reason of his peculiar relations with the Jews at the present time, we have agreed not to disclose his identity nor to give any further details of the Paris meeting beyond the following extracts which, though sometimes freely translated, nevertheless substantially convey the meaning of the original statements.

* * * *

As long as there remains among the Gentiles any moral conception of the social order, and until all faith, patriotism and dignity are uprooted, our reign of the world shall not come...

We have already fulfilled past of our work, but we cannot yet claim that the whole of our work is done. We have still a long way to go before we can overthrow our main opponent: the Catholic Church ...

We must bear in mind that the Catholic Church is the only institution which has stood, and which will, as long as it remains in existence, stand in our way. The Catholic Church, with her methodical work and her edifying and moral teachings, will always keep her children in such a state of mind, as to make them too self-respecting to yield to our domination, and to bow before our future King of Israel ...

That is why we have been striving to discover the best way of shaking the Catholic Church to her very foundations. We have spread the spirit of revolt and false liberalism among the nations of the Gentiles so as to persuade them away from their faith and even to make them ashamed of professing the precepts of their Religion and boeying the Commandments of their Church. We have brought many of them to boast of being atheists, and more than that, to glory in being descendants of the ape! We have given them new theories, impossible realisation, such as Communism, Anarchism, and Socialism, which are now serving our purpose ... The stupid Gentiles have accepted them with the greatest enthusiasm, without realising that those theories are ours, and that they constitute our most powerful instrument against themselves ...

We have blackened the Catholic Church with the most ignominious calumnies, we have stained her history and disgraced even her noblest activities. We have imputed to her the wrongs of her enemies, and have thus brought these latter to stand more closely by our side ... So much so, that we are now witnessing, to our great satisfaction, rebellions against the Church in several countries ... We have turned her Clergy into objects of hatred and ridicule, we have subjected them to the contempt of the crowd ... We have caused the practice of the Catholic Religion to be considered out of date and a mere waste of time ...

And the Gentiles, in their stupidity, have proved easier dupes than we expected them to be. One would expect more intelligence and more practical common-sense, but they are no better than a herd of sheep Let them graze in our fields till they become fat enough to be immolated to our future King of the World ...

We have founded many secret associations, which all work for our purpose, under our orders and our direction. We have made it an honor, a great honor, for the Gentiles to join us in our organizations, which are, thanks to our gold, flourishing now more than ever. Yet is remains our secret that those Gentiles who betray their own and most precious interests, by joining us in our plot, should never know that those associations are of our creation, and that they serve our purpose ...

One of the many triumphs of our Freemasonry is that those Gentiles who become members of our Lodges, should never suspect that we are using them to build their own jails, upon whose terraces we shall erect the throne of our Universal King of Israel; and should never know that we are commanding them to forge the chains of their own servility to our future King of the World.

So far, we have considered our strategy in our attacks upon the Catholic Church from the outside. But this is not all. Let us now explain how we have gone further in our work, to hasten the ruin of the Catholic Church, and how we have penetrated into her most intimate circles, and brought eve some of her Clergy to become pioneers of our cause.

Apart altogether from the influence of our philosophy we have take other steps to secure a breach in the Catholic Church. Let me explain how this has been done.

We have induced some of our children to join the Catholic body, with the explicit intimation that they should work in a still more efficient way for the disintegration of the Catholic Church, by creating scandals within her. We have thus followed the advice of our Prince of the Jews who so widely said: "Let some of your children become canons, so that they may destroy the Church." Unfortunately, not all among the 'convert' Jews have proved faithful to their mission. Many of they have even betrayed us! But, on the other hand, others have kept their promise and honored their word. Thus the counsel of our Elders has proved successful.

We are the Fathers of all Revolutions-even of those which sometimes happen to turn against us. We are the supreme Masters of Peace and War. We can boast of being the Creators of the REFORMATION! Calvin was one of our Children; he was of Jewish descent, and was entrusted by Jewish authority and encouraged with Jewish finance to draft his scheme in the Reformation.

Martin Luther yielded to the influence of his Jewish friends, and again, by Jewish authority and with Jewish finance, his plot against the Catholic Church met with success ...

Thanks to our propaganda, to our theories of Liberalism and to our misrepresentations of Freedom, the minds of many among the Gentiles were ready to welcome the Reformation. They separated from the Church to fall into our snare. And thus the Catholic Church has been very sensibly weakened and her authority of the Kings of the Gentiles has been reduced almost to naught ...

We are grateful to Protestants for their loyalty to our wishes-although most of them are, in the sincerity of their faith, unaware of their loyalty to us. We are grateful to them for the wonderful help they are giving us in our fight against the stronghold of Christian Civilization, and in our preparations for the advent of our supremacy over the whole world and over the Kingdoms of the Gentiles.

So far we have succeeded in overthrowing most of the Thrones of Europe. The rest will follow in the near future. Russia has already worshipped our rule. France, with her Masonic Government, is under our thumb. England, in her dependence upon our finance, is under our heel; and in her Protestantism is our hope for the destruction of the Catholic Church. Spain and Mexico are but toys in our hands. And many other countries, including the U.S.A., have already fallen before our scheming.

But the Catholic Church is still alive ...

We must destroy her without the least delay and without the slightest mercy. Most of the press in the world is under our control; let us therefore encourage in a still more violent way the hatred of the world against the Catholic Church. Let us intensify our activities in poisoning the morality of the Gentiles. Let us spread the spirit of revolution in the minds of the people. They must be made to despise Patriotism and the love of their family, to consider their faith as a humbug, their obedience to the Church as a degrading servility, so that they may become deaf to the appeal of the Church and blind to her warnings against us. Let us, above all, make is impossible for Christians outside the Catholic Church to be reunited with that Church, or for other non-Christians to join that Church; otherwise the greatest obstruction to our domination will be strengthened and all our work undone. Our plot will be unveiled, the Gentiles will turn against us, in the spirit of revenge, and our domination over them will never be realised.

Let us remember that as long as there still remain active enemies of the Catholic Church, we may hope to become Masters of the World ... And let us remember always that the future Jewish King will never reign in the world before the Pope in Rome is destroyed, as well as all the other reigning Monarchs of the Gentiles upon earth.

Author's Note

Before these facts came to my knowledge, I was rather careless in the fulfillment of my religious duties, but since then, my faith, thank God, has grown stronger and stronger, and my belief in the Catholic Church as being the only bulwark against the nemes of our Christian Civilization, has become firmer than ever. That is why I pray that ever Christian be warned against the impending danger of the Jewish plot, so that the whole Christian World may rally under the banner of the Catholic Church, and thus become united against our common, powerful foe.

G.G.

Vision of Pope Leo XIII

On October 13, 1884, after Pope Leo XIII had finished celebrating Mass in the Vatican Chapel, attended by a few Cardinals and members of the Vatican staff, he suddenly stopped at the foot of the altar. He stood there for about 10 minutes, as if in a trance, his face ashen white. Then, going immediately from the Chapel to his office, he composed the prayer to St. Michael, with instructions it be said after all Low Masses everywhere. When asked what had happened, he explained that, as he was about to leave the foot of the altar, he suddenly heard voices - two voices, one kind and gentle, the other guttural and harsh. They seemed to come from near the tabernacle. As he listened, he heard the following conversation:

The guttural voice, the voice of Satan in his pride, boasting to Our Lord: "I can destroy your Church"

The gentle voice of Our Lord: "You can? Then go ahead and do so."

Satan: "To do so, I need more time and more power."

Our Lord: "How much time? How much power?

Satan: "75 to 100 years, and a greater power over those who will give themselves over to my service."

Our Lord: "You have the time, you will have the power. Do with them what you will."

After this vision Pope Leo XIII penned two prayers to Saint Michael. The longer one is reproduced below. It should be noted that he also authorized a general exorcism prayer that is discussed in the next chapter.

Prayer to Saint Michael the Archangel

O glorious Archangel Saint Michael, Prince of the heavenly host, be our defense in the terrible warfare which we carry on against principalities and powers, against the rulers of this world of darkness, spirits of evil. Come to the aid of man, whom God created immortal, made in His own image and likeness, and redeemed at a great price from the tyranny of the devil. Fight this day the battle of our Lord, together with the holy angels, as already thou hast fought the leader of the proud angels, Lucifer, and his apostate host, who were powerless to resist thee, nor was there place for them any longer in heaven. That cruel, that ancient serpent, who is called the devil or Satan who seduces the whole world, was cast into the abyss with his angels. Behold this primeval enemy and slayer of men has taken courage. Transformed into an angel of light, he wanders about with all the multitude of wicked spirits, invading the earth in order to blot out the Name of God and of His Christ, to seize upon, slay, and cast into eternal perdition, souls destined for the crown of eternal glory. That wicked dragon pours out. as a most impure flood, the venom of his malice on men of depraved mind and corrupt heart, the spirit of lying, of impiety, of blasphemy, and the pestilent breath of impurity, and of every vice and iniquity. These most crafty enemies have filled and inebriated with gall and bitterness the Church, the spouse of the Immaculate Lamb, and have laid impious hands on Her most sacred possessions. **In the Holy Place itself, where has been set up the See of the most holy Peter and the Chair of Truth for the light of the world, they have raised the throne of their abominable impiety with the iniquitous design that when the Pastor has been struck the sheep may be scattered.** Arise then, O invincible Prince, bring help against the attacks of the lost spirits to the people of God, and give them the victory. They venerate thee as their protector and patron; in thee holy Church glories as her defense against the malicious powers of hell; to thee has God entrusted the souls of men to be established in heavenly beatitude. Oh, pray to the God of peace that He may put Satan under our feet, so far conquered that he may no longer be able to hold men in captivity and harm the Church. Offer our prayers in the sight of the Most High, so that they may quickly conciliate the mercies of the Lord; and beating down the dragon, the ancient sermon, who is the devil and Satan, do thou again make him captive in the abyss, that he may no longer seduce the nations. Amen.

V/ Behold the Cross of the Lord; be scattered ye hostile powers.

R/ The Lion of the Tribe of Juda has conquered the root of David.

V/ Let Thy mercies be upon us, O Lord.

R/ As we have hoped in Thee.

V/ O Lord hear my prayer.

R/ And let my cry come unto Thee.

V/ Let us pray. O God, the Father of our Lord Jesus Christ, we call upon Thy holy Name, and as suppliants, we implore Thy clemency, that by the intercession of Mary, ever Virgin, immaculate and our Mother, and of the glorious Archangel Saint Michael, Thou wouldst deign to help us against Satan and all other unclean spirits, who wander about the world for the injury of the human race and the ruin of our souls. *R/* Amen.

Truth About The Devil

By: Fr. Dominic Szymanski, O.F.M., Conv.

Influence of the Evil Spirit

The influence of evil spirits in human affairs is far greater than most men are willing to admit. Although God has created all things to His own glory, the "Evil One" exerts all his tremendous powers to frustrate this plan of God by claiming creatures for himself. The almighty God does not stop the "Evil One" any more than He stops a human being from committing murder or any other sin. God triumphs over the malice of the devil by turning evil into good. Adam and Eve sinned in Paradise through the influence of Satan. God did not prevent this sin, but provided a Redeemer who assumed human nature and elevated it above the Angelic Choirs – so much so that the Angels adore the Humanity of Christ. Indeed, God turned this great evil into a greater good. "Ubi abundavit delictum, superabundavit gratia." (Rom. V. 20) The Holy Scriptures clearly depict this influence of the Spirit of Darkness in the beginning of the human race. This same influence of evil intervenes in the life of every human being. God created man to His own image, and claims as His own all who bear this stamp of God's likeness. The devil strives to destroy this "likeness to God" in the human soul by inducing man to sin, and thereby substituting his own likeness. God does not prevent this activity any more than He prevented the fall of Adam. God rules every soul by love; the devil seeks to rule by hate, destruction of grace, and frustration of God's mercy. As God never changes, so also the devil never changes; he always was and always will be the enemy of God, the hater of souls, the father of lies and deceit, and the one through whom death has entered the world. The foregoing is nothing new. No one denies it, but it is also true that few apply it in practical life. As a general rule the sinner will acknowledge the sin, admit his guilt, but will deny all influence of the devil. This denial does not make him more learned; on the contrary, to his own detriment, he fails to understand the entire issue. It would be as though one acknowledged and treated an illness, but neglected to consider the cause of the sickness. In human affairs we both cure the disease and prevent is recurrence. The children of light in their spiritual world should use the same prudence, and both acknowledge sin and recognize its evil instigator. When a sinner at the point of death refuses to be reconciled with God, it is not St. Michael who hardens his heart, but it is the enemy of God and of souls. Exclude the enemy and the hardened sinner will turn to God, with tears and contrition.

Story Of The Hardened Sinner

The following story is an illustration of this. In a certain Illinois city a man lay dying of cancer of the throat which doctors had pronounced as incurable, and had declared that death would follow soon. The good sisters of the hospital in which he was a patient had tried in vain to have him go to confession, sending priest after priest to speak to him. Each priest was treated in the same way. As soon as he would mention confession the sick man simply turned to the wall, saying that there were other sick who wanted to confess their sins, but that it was a waste of time for the priest to talk to him about it, because he did not want to go to confession. The continual insistence of the priests and sisters so angered him that he left the hospital. After a few weeks another hemorrhage occurred, and the family in haste and desperation again sent for a priest, hoping against hope that he would not die without the Sacraments. Two priests of the parish had visited him previously without success, so this time a priest who had had some experience with a number of cases of exorcism went to the sick man. As usual he turned to the wall. The exorcist stood at the foot of the bed and ordered the devil: "I command you, evil spirit, in the name of the Most Holy Trinity, God the Father, God the Son, and God the Holy Ghost, to depart, I command you in the name of our Lord Jesus Crucified to leave this room so that this soul will return to its God and Creator." These words were said secretly. The sick man turned and said, "I do not know how to confess." The answer of the priest was: "I will help you. I will ask you questions, you merely answer yes or no." Once the confession was begun the sick man broke into tears, and made a most humble and contrite confession. The priest then hurried back to the Church and brought him Viaticum. Meanwhile, in the rectory, a spirited debate was in progress among the other fathers. Some maintained that the man was a hardened sinner who would never give in even to the point of death; while others maintained that the exorcist would drive out the devils and make it possible for the sick man to confess. They even made bets on the outcome...those who had greater faith collected. The next morning the poor man died.

The Devil Interferes With Parish Projects

Another illustration of the power of the devils to hinder a good work, and the power of exorcism to render them helpless: A certain priest in North Dakota was trying to introduce Perpetual Adoration into his parish, so that at no time during day or night would the Prisoner of the Tabernacle be alone and unattended. His efforts aroused a storm of objections and criticism. Certain prominent members of the parish objected strenuously to the practice, and loudly claimed that the parish had existed for many years without it, that it was something unheard of, that no other parish practiced it, that the pastor should try to get the careless Catholics to practice their religion with a fair degree of regularity, and leave all that extra-ordinary piety to the cloistered nuns (who did nothing anyway) and had plenty of time for new and strange devotions. The following Sunday the pastor announced to his people before the sermon that he was going to read a special blessing for them, composed by Pope Leo XIII as an antidote against the powers of evil. He asked them to kneel down and join with him in prayer that the powers of evil be diminished, and that the blessing would extend to their homes, their farms, places of business, to the members of their families and to their relatives and friends. He then read the Leonine Exorcism from the Rituale Romanum. Immediately after Mass several of those same men who had opposed the introduction of the practice of Adoration into the parish pledged themselves to make hours of adoration, and use their influence with the members of their families to do the same. All opposition to the practice of Adoration immediately disappeared. It is evident that the objections were overcome by eliminating the objector.

Open Rebellion

Another example of a very practical value of the official prayers of the Church against the devil is the following: A certain young lady told her pastor that she had a very normal desire to marry, that she wanted to have a home and a family as other women had, but that she could not hold any young man, that she seemed to repel rather than attract them. She told of her past experience and admitted that her life was far from being exemplary. The pastor told her that she was rebelling against the will of God, and taking her salvation into her own frail hands, that it was necessary for her to submit to God, that she was trying to live her own life and not the life which God was pointing out to her. She replied: "I have prayed to God, I have made novenas, I even have fasted, and God has no right to deprive me of this human happiness. If God refuses to hear my prayers for a husband I will never submit to Him, I will hate Him eternally." The pastor excused himself for a moment and returned with the ritual and holy water. The girl was asked to kneel down before him, and he recited "The Exorcism." After this was done the girl seemed to be entirely different. With tears of contrition she recited a formula of submission suggested by the pastor, and promised that she would repeat it daily. The strong diabolical influence in this case, and effectiveness of the exorcism, is evident. If you are anxious to save souls of obstinate sinners, recite the exorcisms over them. The power of the devil will be broken and they surely will be converted.

Priestly Powers

To curb the influence of Satan, Christ has given priests necessary powers – the powers of exorcism, but in our days they are buried deep in the ground for fear that sometime they may be used. The servant who buried his talent in the parable of the gospel was called a "wicked and slothful servant" by the Master, and he ordered him to be cast into "the Darkness outside where there will be weeping and gnashing of teeth." Every priest is an exorcist by virtue of his ordination. This power must be used, and used very extensively, with firmness and authority, otherwise the enemy creates havoc among the sheep of God, unmolested even by those who have the duty and the obligation to guard the flock of Christ. Priests should exclude the infernal wolves, not by meekly begging them to depart, but by a firm command. "I command you to depart in the name of our Lord Jesus Christ Crucified." The Church does not ordain priests with the power of forgiving sins only, but she gives them the power to exclude the assassin who is the cause of all sin. The civil government maintains a police force and the Church of God also has the authority to cast into the abyss even the princes and powers of hell who are the prime perpetrators of crime against God.

The Priest Should Not Fear

Good priests should not fear to undertake an exorcism – and by good priests is meant those who habitually live in a state of grace. It is not required that the exorcist be a saint worthy of canonization, or even close to it. If a priest can stand at the altar and offer the Most Holy Sacrifice with a clear conscience, he can also be a successful exorcist. This work is a spiritual one, and Christ stands ready to help whenever our strength falls short. "Behold, I have given you power to tread upon serpents and scorpions, and upon all the power of the enemy; and nothing shall hurt you. (Luke X, 19.)

Valuable Experience

Exorcisms are uplifting and instructive. One exorcism brings us closer to God, and fills our lives with more spirituality than many retreats. One exorcism will teach us more about the devil and his machinations than can be learned from many books.

Fasting

Fasting is necessary. During my own exorcisms I observe a "black fast" (total abstinence from food and drink) for three days, then eat normally for a period of three days, and so on during the entire exorcism. My experience with these fasts is that the first day is the hardest, the second not so hard, and since the fast ends on the third day at 3:00 PM, it is bearable. For those who have no experience with total abstinence from both food and drink for such long periods, I would suggest that they fast for a period of 24 hours only, then eat normally the following day, and fast again on the third day – and so on. Without fasting it is impossible to drive out the devils.

The Stole

A stole about ten feet long should be prepared, one long enough so that it may be tied around the neck of the possessed person and still be long enough to be worn by the exorcist. One end of the stole should be tied around the neck of the person exorcised after the prayer: "Omnipotens Domine, Verbum Dei Patris, etc." has been recited. The prayers of exorcism begin with the Litany of All the Saints, after which are recited the prayers contained in the Roman Ritual in the section entitled "RITUS EXORCIZANDI OBSESSOS A DAEMONIO," and they should be continued without interruption for at least two hours at a time. From eight to ten hours each day should be devoted to the work of exorcising, until the evil spirits have been expelled. The physical condition of the exorcist and the afflicted one should always be considered. Prudence is the best guide. The psalms which follow the rite of exorcism may be omitted and that time devoted to the recitation of the direct prayers contained in the formula itself. The leonine exorcism, which begins with the prayers of St. Michael, may be recited with the longer formula. Once the exorcism has been started it should continue until the possessing evil spirits have been driven out. This may be a matter of hours or days, or of weeks or months; but the length of time is not so important as the fact of expulsion. The exorcist must command the demon to indicate the day and the hour of his departure, and what sign he will give when going out. Generally the demon repeats his name three times before leaving. The exorcist must never place too much reliance on any statement or promise of the demons, but should continue the prayers of exorcism even if the signs of departure have been given, to eliminate the possibility of deception. The devils are liars. They will tell the exorcist that they will not resist any longer, and that they are ready to leave. They will mention their names three times as agreed, the possessed person will appear normal, but all this is often only a maneuver of the devil to deceive the exorcist. For this reason, even after the signs of liberation have been given, the exorcisms should be continued for two or three days. If the devil did not leave he will not be able to remain hidden under the ordeal of exorcism for such a length of time.

The Relief Obtained in Certain Cases

Some possessed persons can hardly be liberated, others will never be completely freed; but even in these cases the exorcism will bring relief. The exorcist should never be discouraged, because even in cases where the afflicted one is never completely freed, great battles are fought against the enemy of God, and his powers are weakened. Such exorcisms might be compared to "delaying actions" in warfare, which are never accompanied by victory, but nevertheless serve an essential purpose in the general plan of battle. It is quite possible and in fact it often happens that relieved persons again become possessed. Such possession cases should be treated the same as any other case of possession.

Causes of Possession

The question: "What causes possession," is often asked, but it cannot be fully answered because some of the causes are known and some are not. The general impression that possessions occur because of an obstinate sinful life may or may not be true in a particular case. Even pious and holy persons have been known to be possessed. The following are some of the causes of possession.

1. FORTUNE TELLERS AND THE LIKE. Those who seek information from fortune tellers and ouija boards, or cures from spiritualists, often become possessed. They seek information, not from God, but from forbidden sources. Hence it is no wonder that the devils enter and give them even more information than they care to have. God complained of Ochozias, the King of Israel: "Is there not a God in Israel that ye go to consult Beelzebub, the god of Accaron?" Some spiritualists effect apparent cures by prayers, but afterward the cured persons are afflicted in other ways day and night. The devil makes them pay a heavy price for services rendered.

2. MALEFICIUM. Maleficium placed in food or drink will cause possession. The devil has his agents who prepare this diabolical substance by which he is able to enter human and animal bodies. In this way even innocent victims may become possessed. The blessing of such food and drink will break the

maleficium and render it harmless. For this reason the Church blesses all things, expelling the evil one, and dedicating them to the purpose for which they were created. The unseen benefits of every blessing will only be known in eternity.

3. CURSING. Cursing by those in authority, especially parents cursing their children, may sometimes cause diabolical possession. Some children have been found to be possessed because their parents directly offered them to the devil even before they were born. On the contrary, in the lives of the saints we find that some were offered to God before their birth. This practice is praise worthy and it should be followed by every Christian mother.

4. DIRECT INVOCATION. Should it ever happen, quod Deus Avertat, that a person would directly give himself to the evil one, possession by the devil would almost certainly follow. God is just, even in His dealings with the devils and as he would recognize the free choice of the creature who would choose Him as a Master, so also will He permit the evil spirits to take possession of those who deliver themselves to the enemy.

5. PERMISSION BY GOD. For the greater glory of God, and for His triumph over His enemies, God sometimes permits that the devil take possession of perfectly innocent people. These are His "Victim Souls," who offer themselves to God to suffer every possible torture in order that sinners may be saved. In such cases there is no question of guilt, or just retribution for faults committed; but such possession is permitted in order that the powers of Hell be weakened and glory be given to God.

The Blessed Sacrament in Exorcisms

The Rituale Romanum cautions that the Blessed Sacrament should not be placed on the head of the possessed, or otherwise brought in contact with him, where there is danger of irreverence. But if this danger does not exist, for example, where the devils use no violence, this caution does not apply; and the Blessed Sacrament can be used. When the Blessed Sacrament is used, it is placed in an ordinary sick call pyx, and held on the head of the possessed by the exorcist. Its effectiveness is remarkable, and it shortens the exorcism.

Holy Water

Holy water is blessed for the purpose of expelling demons. That which is blessed on Epiphany is especially efficacious because it is blessed with all the exorcisms. It should be given to the possessed at regular intervals about every half-hour, or even oftener.

Routine

A good routine to follow during the exorcism is to have the possessed person kneel for fifteen minutes and then be seated for a similar period. A crucifix should be place on the table, and when the time comes to kneel he should adore and kiss the crucifix, and continually pray for his deliverance. If these lines will arouse interest, and help the future exorcist to weaken the power of the devil over God's creatures, they will have served their purpose.

Permission to Exorcise

Exorcism is a command to the demon, given in the name of God to depart from a person, place or thing. The formula of exorcism as given in the Roman Ritual is not reserved. It can be used by anyone, even by a lay person. There is no prohibition forbidding its use and the Church did not reserve those beautiful prayers, exclusively to the Sacred Ministers. Exorcism may be solemn or simple; public or private. The exorcism is solemn if it is performed to expel the demon himself; simple if it is performed to curb the influence of the demon. The Exorcism is public if it is performed by an ordained minister who acts as an Exorcist in the name and by the authority of the Church, in virtue of the powers received in Sacred Ordination. This power over possessed persons cannot be publicly used without special and express permission of the Ordinary. This prohibition is clearly defined in Canon 1151 No. 1: "No one endowed with the power of exorcising is allowed to pronounce an exorcism over a possessed person unless he has obtained special and express permission to do so from the Ordinary." Hence, permission is required for solemn public exorcisms over possessed persons. No permission is needed for solemn public exorcisms over homes, field, animals, to places and in all private and simple exorcisms.

The Ordinary to grant this permissions is the Ordinary in whose diocese the exorcisms are performed or the Ordinary of the Priest. If the priest is an exempt religious his major superior may grant the permission. The Exorcist having obtained the required permission exercises his power received in Sacred Ordination and he acts in the name and authority of the Church, therefore, he must use only the prescribed formula in the Roman Ritual excluding all private formulas, regardless of how pious they may be. The formula prescribed by the Church is self-sufficient, capable of expelling all spirits of darkness, hence private prayers should not be used by the exorcist during the exorcisms. Exorcism is private, if it is performed not in the name and authority of the Church, but in the name of the expelling person. If some good holy layman would undertake to exclude the devil from a possessed person, he would be performing a solemn private exorcism for which no permission is necessary from the Ordinary. The Church restricts the public use of the power of her Ordained Exorcists, not private persons. What is permitted to a lay person cannot be denied to a priest. When the priest acts as a private person, he should not use the exorcism stole. Although public exorcisms performed by the authority of the Church are more effective, nevertheless the demon may also be expelled from possessed persons by private exorcisms. Christ has promised not only to His Apostles but to all who will believe in His Name, that they will cast out the devils. "These signs shall follow them that believe; In my name they shall cast out devils; they shall speak with new tongues; they shall take up serpents; and if they shall drink any deadly thing, it shall not hurt them; they shall lay their hands upon the sick, and they shall recover." (Mark XVI, 17-18.) Exorcisms should be used often, and whenever they are needed. When the permission is necessary, it should be obtained, and Ecclesiastical Superiors are not free to say yes or no. If the case is certain it must be yes, because the Sacramentals cannot be denied to a person who reasonably asks for them. It is a serious infringement of duty and inexcusable sin to leave a person in the power and tyranny of the devil, who torments his victims, day and night. In case of doubt the exorcisms can be recited conditionally, and these trial prayers should be so continued until more definite certitude is obtained. Sacraments are given conditionally, and even greater liberty is permitted with the sacramentals. When the time does not permit the recitation of long formal prayers, as for example, during the sacramental confession, when the confessor notices the danger of a sacrilegious confession or a difficulty in confessing sins, a simple command in his own words pronounced with faith will suffice ... e.g. "I command you, evil spirit, in the name of our Lord Jesus Crucified to depart. Observe and notice the change that will follow.

Use of Exorcism in the Church

Exorcisms are used very extensively in the Church. In the blessing of salt and of holy water, exorcisms are used so that these creatures of God in turn may break the power of the enemy wherever they may be sprinkled, and even put to flight the enemy himself and all his angels. The Church admits the necessity of expelling demons in the ordinary affairs of our every day life. We find water blessed for that purpose at the entrance of every church. This water is blessed the same by priests who are so reluctant to admit the necessity of expelling demons. The Church wants us to sprinkle our homes and everything we use with holy water, to break the power of the devil. Can anyone claim that this diabolical power does not exist? In every baptism the priest uses exorcisms when he says "exi ab eo, immunde spiritus, et da locum Spiritui Sancto Paraclito," and when he says, "Exorciso te, immunde spiritus, in nomine Patris; et Filii; et Spiritus Sancti; ut exeas, et recedas ab hoc famulo Dei (N.). Ipse enim tibi imperat, maledicte damnate, recognosce sententiam tuam, et da honorem Deo vivo et vero, da honorem Jesu Christo Filio eius, et Spiritui Sancto, et recede ab hoc famula Dei (N.), qua istum sibi Deus et Dominus noster Jesus Christus ad suam sanctam tratiam, et benedictionem, fontemque Baptismatis vocare dignatus est." It is a direct command to the evil one to depart. Thus in the blessing of the sick the Church says: "Effugiat ex hoc loco omnis nequitia demonum, adsint Angeli pacis, Donumque hanc deserat omnis maligna discordia." When she blesses sick animals: "Extinguatur in eis omnis diabolica potestas et ne ulterius aegrotent." In the blessing of linens for the sick the priest prays: "Domine Jesu Christe qui ... spiritus nequam ab infirmis easem virtute fugasti sanitatem ... percipere mereantur." The official prayers of the Church admit a diabolical power to produce storms and other disturbances, for she says in the prayers for repelling tempests: "Nibil proficiat inimicus in nobis, et filius iniquitatis non apponat nocere nobis. A domo tua, quaesumus Domine, spiritales nequitiae repellantur, etaerarum discedat malignitas tempestatum." In the blessing of gold, myrrh and incense: "Exorciso te creatura auri, myrrhae et thuris, per Patrem, etc. ... ut a te discedat omnis fraus, dolus et nequitia diaboli, et sis remedium salutare humano generi contra insidias inimici." Again, even in the blessing of the simple and pure flowers of the field on the Feast of the Assumption there is an element of exclusion of diabolical powers: "Concede ut contro diabolicas illusiones et macinationes et fraudes tutamen ferant in quocumque loco positum vel portatum aut habitum aliquid ex eis fuerit." From these references one can read the mind of the Church in the practice of blessing. Blessings have a two-fold purpose; to break the influence of the devil, and to consecrate the object to God. Since the Church in her official prayers and practices admits the influence of evil spirits in the sicknesses of men and of animals, in plants and flowers, and even in inanimate objects, it would be quite presumptuous to hold a contrary opinion. To assert that the evil one has no influence over external objects is in direct opposition to the teachings and practices of the Church. Exorcisms, then, should be recited in sickness, in disaster, and war, in every disturbance, in fact, in everything which brings harm to mankind; over persons who refuse to attend divine services, and over those who are habitually in the state of sin. In all of these cases the influence of the evil one is clearly seen, and Holy Mother Church has provided a clear and efficacious remedy in her prayers against the devil. Exorcisms may be recited at a distance from, and in the absence of, the persons molested. It behooves every Christian, and especially the priests of Christ, to challenge the devil at every turn. The demon is the author of evil, and there is no evil which does not come from him. It is the devil who prompts all disobedience to God's laws, it is he who instills the pride of unbelief, and it is he who sets creatures above God. He is the author of temptations, and were it not for the restraining power of God he would tempt us more than we could stand. God sets a limit that the temptation be not beyond our strength, and gives us power to fight and overcome every temptation. Temptations may arise without the tempter, but very seldom will they end without him. The cunning serpent will take every opportunity to bring about our downfall. "The devil, as a roaring lion, goeth about seeking whom he may devour." (Peter V, 8-9). In the prayers of exorcism in the Roman Ritual the demon is thus addressed: "Audi ergo, et time Satana, inimici fidei, hostis generis humani, mortis adductor, vitae raptor, justitiae declinator, malorum radix, fomes vitiorum, seductor hominum, proditor gentium, incitator invidiae, orgo avaritae, cause discordiae, excitator dolorum, ... exi trangressor. Exi seductor, pleni omni dolo et fallacia, virtutis inimice, inocentium persecutor ... Deus es Filio eius Jesu Christo Domino Nostro, quem tantare ausus es et cricifigere presumpsisti. Tibi et angelis tuis inextinguibile preparatur incendium; quia tu es princeps maledicti homicidii, tu auctor incestus, tu sacrilegorum caput, to actionum pessimarum magister, us hereticorum doctor, to totius obscoenitatis inventor." In these prayers of exorcism the demon is called the enemy of faith, the enemy of the human race, the author of death, snatcher of life, sources of evil, fomentor of vice, origin of avarice, seducer of men, betrayer of nations, instigator of envy, cause of discord, producer of pain, persecutor of the innocent – he who has tempted, and even presumed to crucify, our Lord Jesus Christ. He is called the master of evil, the doctor of heretics and the inventor of all obscenity. Since the Church admits the influence of the evil one in all vices, it follows that the tempter should be curbed and put to flight whenever vice appears. Certainly figs are not found on thorn bushes. Good comes from God – evil comes from the devil. Many sins can be prevented, and much trouble in parishes avoided, by curtailing the activities of the evil one. It is easier to curb the demon than to try to cure the disorders caused by him.

The Devil Should be Exposed

The faults of a community are not secret to anyone. The bad fruit is visible to all, but many fail to see the tree on which it grows, and to recognize the demon as the originator of the evil. The blindness means success to the enemy of salvation. Many a soul would lead a much holier life if the demon were recognized as the source of sin; and sinners would not be so proud of their vices if they knew that they were following the devil, and that he was an actual reality and not a vague enigma, existing only in human fantasy. The Church sees the devil in every evil, and provides a remedy in her numerous blessings and exorcisms; but there are clergymen who, even after many years of experience, do not recognize the instigator of all vice, and will say that they have never seen a person under the influence of the devil. They have seen sinners dying without confession, they have parishioners who have led sinful lives for years, but they will maintain that these are all free agents, that it was all their own doing, and that the sinners alone are responsible. They will absolve the tempter from all blame, and, in effect, defend the enemy. This attitude is not in accordance with the mind of the Church. Such blindness is truly regrettable. The general who would survey a battlefield and view the corpses of his slain soldiers, and still maintain that the enemy had not been there, would be removed because of stupidity. Christ has sent his priests to lead souls to heaven, and when Christ's anointed observe that many souls are slaughtered and lost for eternity, it should not be difficult to conclude that the enemy of God has done this. Show the devil to Christian souls as he really is, and his ugliness will not attract them; hide the devil, and in ignorance they will follow him. The devil has been hidden too long – not by the Church, but by the some who pretend to possess greater wisdom than the Church. The power of the devil vanishes as soon as it is discovered.

Possession

Besides the sporadic influence of evil beings in persons as evidenced by temptations and other evils that come to them, the devil often tries to claim for his own dominion not only men but material objects as well. When persons become possessed the condition is accompanied by various phenomena. They are forced to say and do things quite contrary to their will. They are annoyed and even tortured to an incredible degree. Food and sleep are curtailed. These manifestations differ in every case. Two elements constitute possession: presence of the devil in the body, and dominion exercised by the devil over the body. The devil does not enter the soul; he affects it indirectly through the body.

Signs of Possession

The Roman Ritual mentions three principal signs of possession: speaking unknown tongues or understanding them when used by another, making known hidden and distant facts, exhibiting strength out of proportion with one's age and circumstance. These signs are not by any means exclusive, for the Ritual says: "These and other similar signs, when they occur in great number, are the surest indications of possession." It is quite possible to have a perfect case of diabolical possession without any of the above mentioned signs. The devil is not anxious to prove his presence by speaking unknown tongues or to disclose his identity by marvelous signs. Like the submarine, his power lies in his ability to remain hidden while striking from ambush. On the other hand it is impossible for the devil to possess a person without giving some sign of his presence. If the devil is there he will act. He will assert his dominion over the body by tyranny and torture. He may be able to hide some signs of the possession, but he cannot hide them all. In all cases of possession there are evidences of dual personality – the person himself and the possessing spirit. The physical person will complain of the intrusion of the other, and of the volition of his liberty. He will indicate how he is forced to act by that "something inside of him" contrary to his own conviction and violation. The possessed person will desire to eat, something will stop him; he will desire to pray and that other personality will interfere. These persons did not lose their mind, they know exactly what ails them; they are conscious of another intelligent force within them, which interferes with their freedom. They need help, and that help should be given by those who have the care of souls. It is their duty and obligation to see that these victims of diabolical possession receive the benefit of Sacramentals instituted by the Church for that purpose. It is cruel and unjust to leave them without help.

Procedure

In such cases a prudent priest will ask the afflicted person to kneel and pray and say that he will recite some prayers over him – without mentioning that it is an exorcism. He will recite the Leonine Exorcism, observing well if there be any reaction. If there is, then immediately he should stop the prayer and say: "I command you in the name of the Most Holy Trinity, in the name of God the Father, and of God the Son, and of God the Holy Ghost, tell me your name." It is even better to propose the question in Latin in order that the person afflicted may not be made conscious of his condition. A useful formula is: "Praecipio tibi in nomine Sanctissimae Trinitatis, in nomine Patris +

et Filii + et Spiritus Sancti + dic mihi nomen tuum. Praecipiat tibi Deus Pater + Deus Filius + et Deus Spiritus Sanctus +. Dic mihi nomen tuum." If no reaction be observed, recite the entire exorcism a few times at least, and then propose the questions. If the evil spirit answers, then ask: "How many are with you? How long have you been in this person, and why?" If the priest receives answers to these questions, then there is no longer doubt about the possession. Once the fact of possession has been established, permission of the Ordinary should not be difficult to obtain but gladly given. "Sacramenta et sacramentalia sunt propter homines, et legitime potenti denegari nequent." Bishops are successors of the apostles, sent to spread the Gospel and establish the Kingdom of our Lord Jesus Christ in the souls of men. But to do so the dominion of the devil must be broken, and souls freed from his oppression. Ecclesiastical superiors should beg good priests to undertake this strenuous and hard work of exorcisms – not that the priests should beg them. Frequently it is very difficult to convince the authorities of a possession case and obtain the necessary permission. All priests are exorcists. This was one of the first powers given by the Master to His apostles, and it is one of the first priestly powers given in Holy Orders. If ecclesiastical superiors would tell their priests that they would be called on to undertake cases of possession, and to prepare themselves for it, we would have less skeptics and more piety. This alone would be a very efficient urge to every exorcist to a holy life. The nightly vigil advocated by Father Matteo, and an hour a day before the Blessed Sacrament, would become a universal custom. If, after few recitals of exorcism, no answer is received, it does not mean that there is no possession. In some cases the demon gave answer to the above questions only after ten days of exorcisms. In milder cases the answers are given almost at the very beginning.

Possession Not Rare

Let no one think that possession cases are so rare that it is necessary to go back to the time of Christ to find one. There is no city, not even a single parish, free from cases of possession. This is not a wild assertion made without thought or consideration, but is based on personal experience. I have discovered so many cases of possession that I could not handle them all, even if I worked at them 24 hours a day, every day of the year. The possession of animals is even more frequent. Inanimate objects and articles used for sinful purposes may be possessed. The possessed ouija board will give answers, but if such a board be blessed it will not give any answers. Satan establishes his claim on places and articles of sin, because by sin they have been dedicated to him; just as by blessings of the Church, objects and places are consecrated to God. Hence, it is useful to bless places often. The Church advises that the homes of the faithful be blessed every year. As the state of grace is lost by sin, articles loose their blessing when they are used for sinful purposes, and places become defiled when sins are committed in them. For this reason the Church reconciles Churches and cemeteries when crimes were committed in them. It is a known fact that there were many cases of possession in the time of Our Saviour. Christ is mentioned about thirty times in the Gospels expelling the demon. The Apostles frequently used their powers, and their successors throughout the ages have done the same. Of this we have many examples in the lives of the Saints.

Criticisms

Constructive criticism which throws more light on the subject is welcomed and appreciated, but criticisms based on ignorance and inexperience only multiply the hardships of the exorcist. He should be helped by sacrifice and prayers in a work which so few are willing to undertake, rather than be laughed to scorn by those who do not know. To all skeptics and critics who have no experience in such matters, and only criticize "a priori," there is only one answer: "Your criticism is a contra factum."

Prayer to Saint Michael

Sancte Michaeli Archangele, defende now in praelio contra nequitias et insidias diaboli esto praresidium: Imperet illi Deus, supplices deprecamur, tuque, Princeps militiae caelestis, satanam aliosque spiritus malignos, qui ad perditionem animarum pervaguntur in mundo, divina virtute in infernum detrude. Amen.

Saint Michael, Archangel, defend us in battle. Be our defense against the wickedness and snares of the devil. May God rebuke him, we humbly pray. And you, Prince of the heavenly host, by the power of God, thrust into Hell Satan and the other evil spirits who prowl the world for the ruin of souls. Amen.

Exorcism

This is an English translation of the exorcism prayers inserted in the Roman Ritual by order of Pope Leo XIII. The laity may recite these prayers in order to curb the effects of the Devil.

In the Name of the Father, and of the Son, and of the Holy Ghost. Amen.

Most glorious Prince of the Heavenly Armies, Saint Michael the Archangel, defend us in "our battle against principalities and powers, against the rulers of this world of darkness, against the spirits of wickedness in the high places" (Eph., 6,12). Come to the assistance of men whom God has created to His likeness and whom He has redeemed at a great price from the tyranny of the devil. Holy Church venerates thee as her guardian and protector; to thee, the Lord has entrusted the souls of the redeemed to be led into heaven. Pray therefore the God of Peace to crush Satan beneath our feet, that he may no longer retain men captive and do injury to the Church. Offer our prayers to the Most High, that without delay they may draw His mercy down upon us; take hold of "the dragon, the old serpent, which is the devil and Satan", bind him and cast him into the bottomless pit ... "that he may no longer seduce the nations" (Apoc. 20, 2-3).

In the Name of Jesus Christ, our God and Lord, strengthened by the intercession of the Immaculate Virgin Mary, Mother of God, of Blessed Michael the Archangel, of the Blessed Apostles Peter and Paul and all the Saints. ... we confidently undertake to repulse the attacks and deceits of the devil.

Psalm 67

God arises; His enemies are scattered and those who hate Him flee before Him. As smoke is driven away, so are they driven; as wax melts before the fire, so the wicked perish at the presence of God.

(V) Behold the Cross of the Lord, flee bands of enemies.

(R) The Lion of the tribe of Juda, the offspring of David, hath conquered.

(V) May Thy mercy, Lord, descend upon us.

(R) As great as our hope in Thee.

We drive you from us, whoever you may be, unclean spirits, all satanic powers, all infernal invaders, all wicked legions, assemblies and sects. In the Name and by the power of Our Lord Jesus Christ, + may you be snatched away and driven from the Church of God and from the souls made to the image and likeness of God and redeemed by the Precious Blood of the Divine Lamb. +

Most cunning serpent, you shall no more dare to deceive the human race, persecute the Church, torment God's elect and sift them as wheat. + The Most High God commands you, + He with whom, in your great insolence, you still claim to be equal. "God who wants all men to be saved and to come to the knowledge of the truth" (I Tim. 2,4). God the Father commands you. + God the Son commands you. + God the Holy Ghost commands you. + Christ, God's Word made flesh, commands you; + He who to save our race outdone through your envy, "humbled Himself, becoming obedient even unto death" (Phil.2,8); He who has built His Church on the firm rock and declared that the gates of hell shall not prevail against Her, because He will dwell with Her "all days even to the end of the world" (Matt. 28,20). The sacred Sign of the Cross commands you, + as does also the power of the mysteries of the Christian Faith. + The glorious Mother of God, the Virgin Mary, commands you; + she who by her humility and from the first moment of her Immaculate Conception crushed your proud head. The faith of the holy Apostles Peter and Paul, and of the other Apostles commands you. + The blood of the Martyrs and the pious intercession of all the Saints command you. +

Thus, cursed dragon, and you, diabolical legions, we adjure you by the living God, + by the true God, + by the holy God, + by the God "who so loved the world that He gave up His only Son, that every soul believing in Him might not perish but have life everlasting" (St.John 3, 16); stop deceiving human creatures and pouring out to them the poison of eternal damnation; stop harming the Church and hindering her liberty. Begone, Satan, inventor and master of all deceit, enemy of man's salvation. Give place to Christ in Whom you have found none of your works; give place to the One, Holy, Catholic and Apostolic Church acquired by Christ at the price of His Blood. Stoop beneath the all-powerful Hand of God; tremble and flee when we invoke the Holy and terrible Name of Jesus, this Name which causes hell to tremble, this Name to which the Virtues, Powers and Dominations of heaven are humbly submissive, this Name which the Cherubim and Seraphim praise unceasingly repeating: Holy, Holy, Holy is the Lord, the God of Hosts.

(V) O Lord, hear my prayer. **R.** And let my cry come unto Thee.

Let us pray.

God of heaven, God of earth, God of Angels, God of Archangels, God of Patriarchs, God of Prophets, God of Apostles, God of Martyrs, God of Confessors, God of Virgins, God who has power to give life after death and rest after work: because there is no other God than Thee and there can be no other, for Thou art the Creator of all things, visible and invisible, of Whose reign there shall be no end, we humbly prostrate ourselves before Thy glorious Majesty and we beseech Thee to deliver us by Thy power from all the tyranny of the infernal spirits, from their snares, their lies and their furious wickedness. Deign, O Lord, to grant us Thy powerful protection and to keep us safe and sound. We beseech Thee through Jesus Christ Our Lord. Amen.

(V) From the snares of the devil,

(R) Deliver us, O Lord.

(V) That Thy Church may serve Thee in peace and liberty:

(R) We beseech Thee to hear us.

(V) That Thou may crush down all enemies of Thy Church:

(R) We beseech Thee to hear us. (Holy water is sprinkled in the place where we may be.)

The Real Story Of AA - 1025

By: Yves Dupont

The following true story was originally published in 1972 by Yves Dupont in his magazine <u>World Trends</u>.

The Confession Of Mikolaj
The Antipriest

This man has no name, but we shall call him Mikolaj because he came from Poland where he was born in 1917, perhaps from Russian parents fleeing the Revolution. He was found wandering along a road at the age of three, by a Polish Doctor and his wife, both devout Catholics. The year of his birth must have been determined by the Doctor because the child, who was crying, spoke only a little Polish and a little Russian and did not even know his own name. The Polish couple had no child of their own. They adopted him and loved him as their own son. In his confession, Mikolaj related that his foster parents were very good to him, very generous, full of affection, and that this recollection, even fifty years later, filled him with "seething Anger". For he had been trained, as an agent of the devil, to hate what normal people respect and love. Memories of his childhood were like intruders trying to move his heart and bring about his conversion. He could not bear them, he had to hate them, and hate also those who were responsible for these sweet memories. The child grew into a boy of quiet disposition and studious habits. His intelligence and capacity for learning appear to have been extraordinary, and so was his ambition. The latter seems to have played an important part in his downfall at the age of 14 or 15 when, one evening, shortly before a planned visit to Rome and Paris, he overheard his parents express their concern about his passport and his legal status as an adopted child. He was shattered! He had been brought up to believe that these two were really Mother and Father to him, and to discover this was not the truth was a great shock to him. He could not get over it. They died in his heart as effectively as if they had died physically. They ceased to be "Mum and Dad". They became "Those People". Distracted almost out of his mind, he fled from the house immediately. He decided to leave Poland, and made for the Russian border. A schoolmate of his had an uncle in Russia, in Leningrad to be precise, where he was as a high ranking public servant. A few days later, with a letter of introduction in his hand, he called at the uncle's home in Russia. The uncle noticed his alertness, intelligence and ambition, and was favorably impressed.

"If you wish to succeed, my lad," he told him, "first of all you must study some foreign languages and absorb the doctrine of the Party."

For the next six years, Mikolaj studied furiously and absorbed the Marxist doctrine in its entirety. The uncle, as he soon found out, was a high ranking official in the Secret Police. There is little doubt that his interest for the young man had been aroused by considerations which had little to do with affection or sympathy. The boy was highly intelligent, had no parents or relative to divide his allegiance or interfere with his Marxist studies, and he was ambitious. In fact, the perfect raw material with which to form a good agent. Other factors, too, contributed to this. Mikolaj had an enormous capacity for work, a remarkable memory, and he despised all women and the "fools" who love them too much. This would exclude emotional involvements with the fair sex.

The six years of study completed, Mikolaj, now 20, was called to the office of the Uncle who told him point blank:

"I am going to send you abroad to become a militant atheist on the world scene. Your main duty will be to fight all religions, but the Catholic religion in particular because of its efficient structures. In order to achieve this you will enter a seminary and become a Catholic priest. But you must return to Poland and seek reconciliation with your foster parents who will be delighted to hear of your "vocation" and who will help you to become a priest."

Mikolaj had mixed feelings. The idea of being a secret agent filled him with elation, but the command to see his "parents" again and act the part of a loving son for the six long years which he would spend in the seminary, was abhorrent to him. Self control is one of the qualities of a secret agent. In this case, however, Mikolaj could not quite conceal his feelings even after 6 years of training in Marxist schools. The Uncle remarked on this, which had Mikolaj blush, and drew a further remark from the Uncle:

"A secret agent does not blush, has no blood in his veins, has no heart, loves no one not even himself. He is the Thing of the Party, and the Party can devour him alive and without warning. Wherever you are, get it into your head that you will be watched. At the first sign of weakness we shall get rid of you. And, of course, if you are in danger, do not rely on us. You will be disavowed."

Answered Mikolaj: "I know all this very well, but I beg to ask why I should show love and affection to my false parents when I feel nothing but hatred for them."

"Hatred has no room in our service, except the hatred of God following Lenin's example. We kill without hatred simply to serve the Party. You must see your parents again, but you will not enter a Polish seminary. You will be sent overseas, perhaps to Canada, where discipline is not as strict as in Europe, and there is less likelihood of discovery. Besides, with that madman now in Germany we have every reason to fear a war in Europe."

The Uncle gave him further instructions and reminders: "Persecution is useless. We don't want any martyrs as long as we are not in complete control of the West. Religion must be destroyed by dialectics. [Dialectic: The art or practice of examining statements logically as by question and answer.] You are to send me a report every week. After a while you will be put in touch with the rest of the network and you will be responsible for ten other agents, but you will not know who they are, and they will not know you. To reach them and to reach you everything will go through this office. We already have many priests in those countries which are afflicted with Catholicism, one is a bishop. We have observers everywhere. Some, especially trained for the purpose, scan the newspapers of the whole world every day and send us reports on the development of ideas in the West. Our foreign policy is based on these. Thus we will be able to see how effective your own work is. You will have to spread new ideas. Ideas that may appeal to some stupid pen pusher who will take them up and publicize them. **No one is more vain than a writer.** Give him an idea, and he will say that it is his own, write about it, enlarge upon it, and thus further our aims. We rely a great deal on writers and journalists. There is no need for us to train them, they work for us without realizing it. You will receive letters from us. You will recognize every letter as genuine by the code numbers SS 1025, which is your own. SS means Seminary Student. **Yes, there are 1024 others.**"

The next few days Mikolaj spent most of his time studying a few confidential files the Uncle had given him. Before he left Russia, a number of further interviews with the Uncle took place. During one of these he told the Uncle of his own ideas on how best to combat religion in the West. An open and bitter opposition had already been ruled out. Persuasion through dialectics, lectures, debates, dialogues and colloquies was the latest method favored by Moscow, and it was to develop considerably after World War II. In almost all such talks the Communist speakers, who were highly trained dialecticians, outsmarted their opponents and often silenced them completely, thus winning many "converts" in the audience. Press reports of such talks further helped to spread Marxist ideas and lent respectability to the Communists who, it was thought, had become "reasonable". The method has indeed proved extremely successful. The penetration of Marxist thinking in the West is now so thorough that echoes of it are quite a common occurrence even in the Catholic press. To complement this method, however, **Mikolaj had devised a more sinister scheme primarily designed to change Catholic doctrine.** Briefly, instead of combating the religious feeling of the people, it consisted in exalting it in a wrong direction and towards some unrealistic objective. The Uncle who, at first had seemed somewhat amused, now listened with great interest (decidedly, he thought, this young man is above average).

Mikolaj went on: "We must put it into their heads, and especially priests, that the time has come to seek and **work for the merging of all religions**. We must, in particular, promote among Catholics a feeling of guilt concerning the "One Truth" which they claim they alone possess. We must convince them that this attitude is a monstrous sin of pride, and that they must now seek reconciliation with other religions. This thought must be made to grow and be uppermost in their minds."

Answered the Uncle: "Very well! But don't you think that this scheme is somewhat unrealistic?"

"Not at all!" said Mikolaj, "I myself was a Catholic up to the age of 15, and a very devout one at that. I think it should be comparatively easy to convince Catholics that there are holy persons among Protestants, Mussulmans [Muslims] and Jews. And since they are holy, they also are the members of the "Communion of Saints" in which Catholics believe. Starting from this, we will say that to keep these people out of the Church is an insult to God. Of course, we shall drop the term "Communion of Saints". We shall substitute for it some other expression such as "Community of Believers" or "People of God". **This will shift the accent from the supernatural to the natural, from the heavenly to the earthly, which is what we want. The whole Catholic terminology can and must be changed.** To those who object we shall reply that the meaning has not changed and that we must adapt our expressions to the modern way of thinking, which is what progress is about. And since Catholic intellectuals, like most intellectuals, seek and value the praise of others, they will be mortally afraid of being "behind the times". they will accept the new terms and promote them among the ignorant people. There is a whole area to be investigated here. I can do no more than outline the plan."

"And how do you envision that Universal Church to which you would have everyone rushing in to?"

"That new Church must be simple. The concept of God must be vague, general and impersonal, not entailing any definite obligations, not demanding sacrifices, and, of course, not providing any inspiration to the people. The universal brotherhood of men must be emphasized above all things. It should not be difficult to persuade Catholics that the Commandment "Love they neighbor as thyself" requires no less than that. In order to make them forget God, **we must get them to worship the human race.** This, however, is a long term effort: it may take 20, 30, or even 50 years.[2] We must be prepared to wait, but I am confident that we shall succeed."

"Very well, we shall examine your idea. Come back next week and we shall give you our reply. Meanwhile, get ready for your departure for Poland".

The following week Mikolaj called at the Uncle's office as arranged. The Uncle told him that his Chief was here and wanted to meet him. Mikolaj was overjoyed, for it was obvious that such a powerful Official would not come merely to signify his refusal. He must have been favorably impressed. Completely self possessed, Mikolaj met

---

[2]   1937 + 20 years = 1957
        1937 + 30 years = 1967
        1937 + 50 years = 1987

the great Chief. However, he instantly disliked his appearance which was one of gross brutality and vulgarity. He reflected that this must be the sort of man who enjoys watching the most cruel tortures in prisons: a true sadist. Mikolaj was above all an intellectual. He disliked the idea of torture which he saw as a mark of weakness and stupidity on the part of the torturer. The Chief looked at him in a manner that bore right through him. Mikolaj felt uneasy. Point blank, the Chief asked: "What do you have most at heart?"

"The victory of the Party," said Mikolaj.

"Good! From today onwards you will be on the roll of our active agents. You will have responsibilities, you will issue orders. But make no mistake about it. We expect to see the fruits of your work in newspapers, books and theological reviews. It is up to you. We have a specialist team of readers whose function it is to analyze the religious writings of the whole world. We will watch your progress. However, I am confident that you will be able to handle this."

Mikolaj reflected that this brute, after all, was no fool. He had correctly assessed his exceptional ability and his outstanding intelligence of which he never doubted himself. He felt completely sure that he would succeed, for he knew well the weak spot of Catholics, which is Charity. With "Charity" it is always possible to instill remorse in the hearts of people, and a remorseful person is inevitably in a state of lesser resistance and, therefore, of higher receptivity to alien ideas and suggestions. This is psychologically certain, just as certain as pure mathematics. With "Charity" it will be possible to persuade Catholics it is a sin to criticize Protestants, Jews, and Mussulmans [Muslims], and that to criticize their beliefs is, in fact, the same as criticizing them. **Thus, Catholics will gradually accept the beliefs of the other religions and their own faith will wane.** The honesty and scruples of Catholics, Mikolaj thought, is the opening through which we shall enter their fortress. It is the fault in the rock that can be plugged with explosives, the weakness which makes a dialogue with them extremely rewarding. A few days later, Mikolaj was back in Poland. He somewhat dreaded his first meeting with his foster father, so he arranged to come "home" when the Doctor was likely to be out. He rang the door bell, and it was his foster mother who came and opened the door. Here is the account of his return:

"She had aged considerably, she did not have any makeup on. She looked ill. She began to shake with emotion, then she cried. Really, women are no good except locked up in harems for the convenience of men in their necessities. Naturally, I begged her to pardon me. That was part of the game. But I knew that this business would be promptly settled, so overcome with joy would she be. Thus, I would not have to abase myself before my foster father when he came home. To see me as a priest of God must have been her most cherished dream. So, without any more ado, I told her of my "irresistible" vocation. The old goose was so happy that she nearly fainted. From then on she would have believed anything I said. And when was I for the first time aware of the "call of God"? Well, I said, it all came suddenly through an apparition. (I had not intended to tell her anything like that, but the idea came to me there and then. I knew this sort of thing would appeal to her, and it amused me anyway). Of course, the Doctor was rather suspicious of the supernatural, but that did not matter, on the contrary, any disagreement between the two could only strengthen my own position, and while they were arguing how my vocation came about, **it would not occur to them that I may not have had any vocation at all**. So I told her in great detail my story of that wonderful heavenly visitation. I said St. Anthony of Padua had come to me, and, to make the picture even nicer, I added that he was carrying the Infant Jesus in his arms. The silly old cow was near to ecstasy. Just then, however, the Doctor arrived and I was relieved to be able to speak to a sensible person after all that nonsense, but I saw immediately that he would have nothing of my story. Never mind! That will make the game even more exciting. The next day we went to see the bishop. He was kind, but reserved. That was just what I had expected. I knew very well that he would not send me to the seminary the next day! My perseverance would prove that my vocation was genuine. Throughout the interview I assumed an air of perfect humility with my eyes cast down except when I was spoken to. He advised me to go and see a Religious Priest who was known for his ability to "discern the spirits". This jargon means that the fellow was supposed to read people's hearts! So I went to see him. Our interview was a protracted one, and I did not like the character. He spoke slowly, deliberately and his speech was punctuated with long, heavy pauses that were rather unpleasant. Of course, I said nothing of my "apparitions". My mother would have most certainly told him already, and my reserve in this respect would look very edifying indeed. I played the part of a very humble young man, and I am sure that I played it most excellently. However, I took some pride in confessing to him that I had never known any girl or woman, and that I was not at all interested in the weaker sex which, in my opinion, has no other function than that of childbearing. I felt sure that he would condone such an outburst of juvenile pride, and it would show him how earnest I was. The "holy" man, however, set a few traps for me. He tried to pin me down on some contradictions. How childish! I was fully trained for that sort of thing. He also asked me why I left my foster parents six years earlier, and why I had never written to them. I thought it would be best not to attempt to justify my past behavior. On the contrary, an admission of human weakness was more likely to move his heart. So I told him in quavering tones that this folly of mine would be the remorse of my whole life. But, I added, the immense sorrow which I caused to my "dear" mother would be more than repaid by the lasting bliss of my priestly vocation, for nothing could make her more happy than that. He agreed, and I now felt certain that he would not have the heart to deprive my aging mother of such great happiness. Our conversation grew more and more friendly as the hours went by, and, when we parted, we were like two old friends. Because of this I was thunderstruck when, a few days later, the bishop told me quietly that, in this priest's opinion, I did not have a vocation. **It was as though the earth had split under my very feet.** I reported the setback to the Uncle through a priest agent who had been appointed to that function. The reply came promptly and it was a terse one:

"Destroy the obstacle."

After pondering a few days on the best way to "destroy the obstacle", a task which I did not relish, I decided to put to good use the special training in bare hand combat which I had received in Russia. But it would be better if this took place outside the priest's monastery. I arranged through my comrade the priest agent that he should invite the Religious to his home. And so it was done. I had felt humiliated and angry at having been rejected by the old coot, and when our second interview took place, I demanded to know his reasons. He calmly answered that he did not have any reason himself, but that the Lord had given him the "discerning of spirits" (I Cor.12:10). I could see that the man was not pretending, he really believed what he said, but his wholly unscientific reason did not satisfy me. How can you argue with a man who believes in magic? **Even his seraphic smile irritated me. That old man behaved like a child.** I told him that I would not hesitate to kill him if this could help me to enter the seminary. **He answered quietly that he knew this.** I was flabbergasted! For a long moment we looked at each other without saying a word. Then he broke the heavy silence and said slowly:

"**You know not what you are doing.**"

"I must confess that I felt then extremely uncomfortable. **This man could read my mind. He possessed powers which I did not understand.** My comrade the priest, who was in the room, sensed that I was faltering. He signaled to me discreetly. In a flash I realized that I was finished unless I carried out the Uncle's orders there and then. I sprang to my feet and with two neat karate blows I killed the old man. In 1938, very few people in the West knew the possibilities afforded by this Japanese art, and I was grateful to my Russian masters for teaching me how to kill "cleanly". Those two blows had caused his heart to stop, and his death would be normally diagnosed as a heart failure. The next day, however, I had a rash all over my body, a symptom of emotional stress. How stupid of me! I was fully confident now that I would eventually enter the seminary, and I was already making plans for the future especially as regard my work for the Party. **I was to inject into Catholic thinking a whole set of new values and a new train of thought.** I was to foster remorse in their hearts, a gnawing sense of guilt, quoting the Gospel: "Be One as the Father and I are One." That sense of guilt must grow into an obsession to the point of rehabilitating Martin Luther. They will be made to believe that schisms and heresies were caused by their own intransigence, that the time had come for them to atone and make reparation by throwing their arms open to their Protestant brethren and confessing their own sin of pride and stubbornness. Of course, we shall not tamper with the Creed except for the word "Catholic" which must be changed to "Universal" or "Christian" as the Protestants use. But we shall not use the name of God except when necessary. We shall speak of man, stress his dignity and nobility. **We must transform the language and thinking pattern of every Catholic.** We must foster the mystique of the human race. At first, we shall say that God exits, but we shall point out that God remains forever outside the field of human experience, and experience is what counts for sensate beings. We shall lay much stress on experience and sensory perceptions. The positive, the experimental and the sensorial must be the basis of the new thinking. We shall say that, since God is invisible, the best way to serve Him is to set up a universal Church in which all men can meet as brothers in mutual goodwill, love, and understanding. This new mystique must finally obfuscate the concept of God of whom we shall speak less and less, **except for saying that we are God** because God is in everyone of us. In this manner, we shall redirect the religious yearnings and superstitions of the people. We shall deify Man. Once Catholics have accepted this new mystique, we shall tell them to strip their churches bare of statues and ornaments because these things are unessential and abhorrent to their dear Protestant and Jewish brethren. Thus all symbols of Catholic worship and devotion will go by the boards, and when they are gone devotions will go too. Yes, we shall promote an iconoclastic zeal especially among the younger generation. They themselves will destroy that jumble of statues, pictures, vestments, reliquaries, organs, etc. It would be a good idea, too, to spread a "prophecy" that says:

"You shall see married priests, and **you shall hear the Mass in the language of the people.**"

This should make our task easier. **We shall incite women to assert their right to the priesthood**, and we shall make the Mass more popular by allowing home Masses that can be said by the father or the mother of the family. Once this practice is established we shall campaign for the abolition of the parish system as antiquated and not in keeping with the needs of modern times. Churches can then be turned into museums, meeting halls, theaters, storerooms and other useful functions. All sorts of exciting ideas came surging into my head, and I coded my whole program before sending it to Moscow. Looking back on these days, I now feel a legitimate pride at having been the first to suggest these ideas to the Party. It is now plain that these were the right ideas, far superior to a mere dialectical attempt at destroying religious belief. Some time later, an order came from Moscow:

"New assignment: go to Rome."

And so I left Poland for what was going to be my lifetime work. Once in Rome I met a priest professor who was in our network. He was a scholar and a scriptural expert. He was then busy preparing a new English version of the Bible, but his work was still secret. In that new version the old cliches about the Virginity of Mary, the Real Presence and like fables were to be adroitly amended and reinterpreted. Instead of "Virgin" Mary will be called "maid". The "brethren" of Jesus will become His "brothers". The "Real Presence" will be explained as a feeling, or experience, when "Christians are gathered together in His name". The notion of "gathering" is an important one to promote the community spirit. Those who do not conform to the Group will be reproved as trouble makers and bad Christians. We must absolutely stifle individual attitudes if we are to control the Group as we please, and the control of the Group is essential for the establishment of Communism. The professor also taught me a sensible way to say Mass since, within six years, I shall be obliged willy nilly to say it also. He never actually pronounced the words of the Consecration. He simply muttered some words that sounded like it. This was possible since the Rubrics require that the words be said in a low voice. Later, of course, the Mass will be radically modified. We shall play down the sacrificial aspect, we shall exalt it as a meal taken by the Community. In case some reactionary priests refuse to conform, and insist on saying the old prayers, we shall direct that the Canon in its entirety be said aloud. This will also make it possible for the people to say the words with the priests, and once this is possible we shall rule that it is indispensable also. Thus the Mass will cease to be the privilege of the priest alone. **The professor was already working on a draft for a New Order of the Mass, and he urged me to do likewise because, he said, it was greatly desirable that we should give the people different kinds of Masses. This will help destroy unity, the mainstay of Catholic power. All this would be a great deal easier if we succeeded in having one of our agents elected as pope.** Failing this, however, we would probably be able to sway the Cardinals sufficiently to obtain the election of a progressive pope who will ratify whatever our agents put on his desk in the name of progress. I was fascinated by the things the professor told me, and I tried to elicit from him the names of some of the other priests and seminarians who were members of our network, but he said he knew little about it. He did say, however, that we had a few professors teaching in the Roman seminaries, and he gave me the name of another professor, a Frenchman, who was giving singing lessons in Rome. He was a member of the Communist Party, and I was told that I could trust him completely. I later met him and befriended him. One day, as we were strolling through the streets of Rome, he said:

"Imagine this city without a cassock in sight. How wonderful it would be!"

"Yes," I nodded, "the cassock must go. After all, they could say Mass in a jacket or jumper!"

"From my Catholic upbringing I understood how vocations often assert themselves in young children: in his cassock, the priest stands out as a man different from the rest. The child likes him and wants to emulate him. But destroy the cassock, and you will destroy the priest. In this way many vocations will die in the bud."

"The merging of all religions," continues Mikolaj in his confessions, "and the brotherhood of man, must always be reasserted as the basic motivation for all the changes. "Love thy neighbor as thyself" will be our scriptural justification. **The greatest change, and the most desirable one, is the suppression of the papacy**, but this appeared very difficult to me in view of Christ's promise: "Thou art the Rock, and upon this Rock I shall build My Church". **We shall therefore endeavor to undermine the authority of the pope in every possible way**, and we shall try to enlist his (the pope's) cooperation to introduce the changes that will make this possible. We shall promote the concept of Episcopal Equality and the priesthood of the laity. When the bishops are elected by the people, and the pope is no more than the president of the bishops, our victory will be near at hand. When, moreover, the parish system has been destroyed through the proliferation of home Masses celebrated **by lay folk in their capacity as "priests", the Mass itself will cease to be.** When, finally, the bishops elected by the people are admitted to vote in a conclave, then the papacy will be in our hands. All must be done in the name of love. Also in the name of love, we shall promote the idea that God is far too loving to want His only Son to die a cruel death for us and to want to create an everlasting hell. Christ will be described as a good man and great revolutionary, and hell as a superstition of the Dark Ages. **We shall no longer mention sin,** and Angels will be relegated to the realm of mythology and fairy tales. Once the people cease to fear God, they will soon forget Him. Our task is to promote these ideas among the Catholic elite via the theological journals which we control, and they in turn will promote them in the Church as their own ideas. **We shall also encourage many new translations of the Bible. The greater the number of translations,**

the better. It will help to create confusion. The number of Catholic scholars who are itching to produce their own versions - undoubtedly the best ever produced in their own eyes - is not lacking. All they need is a little prodding from us. We are faced with a huge task. Many problems remain to be solved: the Rosary, Lourdes, and the twenty odd feasts of Mary are annoying things, but we shall be patient. In any case, we will have to draw up a new calendar and dispose of many Marian feasts as well as many other Saints. The new calendar must look as bare as the table on which **they will say the new Mass.** Such is the substance of the orders which I issued to the network. **The following year I began to work on the draft of a new catechism which would be acceptable to all believers.** It must be practical, human, non committal, and ambiguous. It must stress the humanity of Christ who, in fact, was a brother of ours. But the word "charity" is to be banished absolutely. We shall say "love" instead. Love can be many things, but charity has an intolerable religious connotation. We shall say, of course, that it means the same and the change is more conformable to modern usage. Concerning the precepts of the Church, we shall say that Christians are now fully mature and adult, that the precepts were necessary when the people were ignorant and uneducated, but that it is more fitting to adult Christians to let their own consciences decide. **God, in any case, is far too great and remote to worry about our eating meat on Fridays!** Private confession is a waste of time. We shall promote a communal penitential rite with emphasis on sins committed against our brothers. **The precept of Sunday attendance will be modified too.** We shall say that, because of the working conditions in this modern age, people need their Sunday to relax in the countryside away from the city's fumes. **They should be allowed to attend Mass on Saturday, even on Friday.** God did not say what day was to be reserved. In all cases we shall stress the primacy of the individual conscience over set rules and petty precepts which are unworthy of an adult man and an insult to his dignity. We shall retain the "Our Father" for the time being, but we shall replace "Thee" by "You" and we shall find suitable substitutes for such words as "forgive, temptations, trespasses" and other similar nonsense. The seven sacraments will receive our special attention. The first I would like to abolish is baptism, but it will have to stay for a while. We shall say that Original Sin is not the sin of Adam and Eve who, in any case, never existed. We shall reinterpret it. Baptism, then, will merely be a ceremony marking the coming of a new member into the human brotherhood. We shall do likewise with every Sacrament. Concerning marriage, it shall not be refused to those priests who wish to receive it. In the Mass, the words "Real Presence" and "Transubstantiation" must be deleted. We shall speak of "Meal" and "Eucharist" instead. We shall destroy the Offertory and play down the Consecration and, at the same time, we shall stress the part played by the people. In the Mass, as it is today, the priest turns his back to the people and fills a sacrificial function which is intolerable. He appears to offer his Mass to the great Crucifix hanging over the ornate altar. **We shall pull down the Crucifix, substitute a table for the altar, and turn it around so that the priest may assume a presidential function**. The priest will speak to the people much more than before. To achieve this, we shall shorten what is now called the Mass proper, and we shall add many readings to what is called the Foremass. **In this manner the Mass will gradually cease to be regarded as an act of adoration to God, and will become a gathering and an act of human brotherhood.** All these points will have to be elaborated in great detail and they may take anything up to 30 years before they are implemented, but I think that all my objectives will be fulfilled by 1974. Thus I labored for twenty long years. Pius XII died in 1958. When John XXIII announced a new council, my interest was greatly stimulated. **I reported to my chiefs that this was perhaps the last battle: no effort should be spared**. They were obviously of the same opinion because they immediately appointed me to the highest position in the West European network, and they gave me unlimited financial backing through our Bank in Switzerland. Hearing that Pope John had appointed a commission to draw the schemas of the forthcoming Council, I immediately started to work on counter schemas with the help of avant garde theologians who had been won over to our way of thinking. Thanks to my contacts I managed to obtain copies of the projected papal schemas. They were terrible! I was in a cold sweat! If these schemas are carried, my work of 20 years will have been in vain. I hastily put the finishing touch to my counter schemas, and I circulated them. Eventually, they were tabled in the Council. Thanks to the cooperation of some bishops whose thinking had been conditioned previously, the majority of bishops, reactionary but ill prepared, were completely disconcerted by the highly efficient and coherent interventions of our friends. Most of my counter schemas were carried. But I am not satisfied: many of my schemas, although they were accepted, have been watered down by Pope Paul himself in contempt of the majority vote at the Council. Fortunately, the revised versions contain many ambiguities. **In this manner, it will be possible to initiate further changes, alleging that they are in the spirit of the Council.** At any rate, Pope Paul is a progressive and a humanist. It should not be difficult to manipulate him and obtain sweeping changes in the near future. However, we must begin to work for Vatican III even now. Vatican III, as I see it, will mean the destruction of the Church and the death of God. **Then, I shall come forward, not to nail Christ upon His Cross, but God Himself into His coffin.**"

Concluding Thoughts

In the opening we quoted Pope Pius X warning that the Enemies of the Church were already lying hid within the Church, which confirms what is said in <u>The Permanent Instruction of the Alta Vendita</u>. In other words, their conspiracy was already successful over a century ago, but the ends not yet achieved. We see further proof in the story of Seminary Student 1025, which details the Communist infiltration of the Catholic Church with the same goals as the Freemasons noted above. All three conspiracies have the same goal as the Freemasons, quoted above: "Our final end is that of Voltaire and of the French Revolution, the destruction for ever of Catholicism." It can be seen they want a Catholicism, which is different from that founded by Jesus Christ.

You can see in the Conspiracy, for these are not three separate conspiracies, but three branches of one Conspiracy, that ultimate led by Lucifer himself, the goal of *striking the shepherd*, that is the Pope. Pope Leo XII penned: "In the Holy Place itself, where has been set up the See of the most holy Peter and the Chair of Truth for the light of the world, they have raised the throne of their abominable impiety with the iniquitous design that when the Pastor has been struck the sheep may be scattered." Destroy the Papacy and you destroy the Catholic Church. As <u>The Permanent Instruction of the Alta Vendita</u> puts it: "That which we ought to demand, that which we should seek and expect, as the Jews expected the Messiah, is a Pope according to our wants."

Two things indicate, when this all may happen. Saint Pius X said in his first Encyclical: "So extreme is the general perversion that there is room to fear ... that the Son of Perdition, of whom the Apostle speaks, has already arrived on earth." Pope Leo XIII had his vision on October 13, 1884, thirty three years to the day before the Miracle of the Sun at Fatima. Satan asked for seventy-five to a hundred years to complete his task, which would be between 1959 and 1984. And Seminary Student 1025 said it might take a half a century: "This, however, is a long term effort: it may take 20, 30, or even 50 years." This would mean the job would be completed by 1987.

Are we sitting after these catastrophic events, as described above awaiting the triumph of the Immaculate Heart of Mary promised at Fatima? Something to consider as you heed Jesus' advice from the

Gospels to those in the time of the Great Apostasy: "Let he who reads, understand.

Recommended Books For Further Study

Those who wish to make a more in depth study may find the following books useful:

Antichrist An Historical Review by James Ratton. This book from the 1800's give a unique view of the Great Pope and Great Monarch as well as Antichrist. Many are waiting for the Great Pope and Monarch who appear before Antichrist. According to Ratton they both appeared in the 19th century, so there is nothing baring Antichrist from coming.

The Christian Trumpet by Gaudentius Rossi is another lesser know work on Catholic Prophecy from the late 19th Century.

End of the Present World and the Mysteries of the Future Life by Fr. Charles Arminjon.

The Apocalypse Of St. John by Fr. E. Sylvester Berry. This is a lesser known commentary on the Apocalypse the students of prophecy will find valuable.

The Book of Destiny by Herman Bernard Kramer. This is a more well known commentary on the Apocalypse.

The Prophets and Our Times by Fr. R. Gerald Culleton.

The Reign of Antichrist by Fr. R. Gerald Culleton. These two books have long been in reprint and are used by many to discern prophecy.

Catholic Prophecy: The Coming Chastisement by Yves Dupont. This book was written about the same time Dupont reported the story of Seminary Student 1025, which is reproduced above.

54 Years that Changed the Catholic Church, which details how these prophecies may have already been fulfilled.

Christ the King Library
Delia, Kansas 66418

Made in the USA
Lexington, KY
26 May 2015